BRIDGING JAPANESE/ NORTH AMERICAN DIFFERENCES

Communicating Effectively in Multicultural Contexts

Series Editors: William B. Gudykunst and Stella Ting-Toomey

Department of Speech Communication
California State University, Fullerton

The books in this series are designed to help readers communicate effectively in various multicultural contexts. Authors of the volumes in the series translate relevant communication theories to provide readable and comprehensive descriptions of the various multicultural contexts. Each volume contains specific suggestions for how readers can communicate effectively with members of different cultures and/or ethnic groups in the specific contexts covered in the volume. The volumes should appeal to people interested in developing multicultural awareness or improving their communication skills, as well as anyone who works in a multicultural setting.

Volumes in this series

1. **BRIDGING JAPANESE/NORTH AMERICAN DIFFERENCES**
   William B. Gudykunst and Tsukasa Nishida

2. **INTERCULTURAL COMMUNICATION TRAINING:**
   An Introduction
   Richard W. Brislin and Tomoko Yoshida

3. **EFFECTIVE COMMUNICATION IN MULTICULTURAL**
   HEALTH CARE SETTINGS
   Gary L. Kreps and Elizabeth N. Kunimoto

Bridging Japanese/North American Differences

William B. Gudykunst
Tsukasa Nishida

SAGE Publications
International Educational and Professional Publisher
Thousand Oaks   London   New Delhi

For information address:

 SAGE Publications, Inc.
2455 Teller Road
Thousand Oaks, California 91320

SAGE Publications Ltd.
6 Bonhill Street
London EC2A 4PU
United Kingdom

SAGE Publications India Pvt. Ltd.
M-32 Market
Greater Kailash I
New Delhi 110 048 India

Printed in the United States of America

Library of Congress Cataloging-in-Publication Data

Gudykunst, William B.
    Bridging Japanese/North American differences / William B. Gudykunst, Tsukasa Nishida.
        p. cm. − (Communicating effectively in multicultual contexts; 1)
    Includes bibliographical references and index.
    ISBN 0-8039-4834-4. − ISBN 0-8039-4835-2 (pbk.)
    1. United States−Relations−Japan. 2. Japan−Relations−United States. 3. Intercultural communication−United States.
4. Intercultural communication−Japan. I. Nishida, Tsukasa, 1948-.
II. Title. III. Series.
E183.8.J3G93 1994
303.48'273052−dc20   93-43671

94 95 96 97 98 10 9 8 7 6 5 4 3 2 1

Sage Production Editor: Astrid Virding

Contents

Preface

We became interested in Japanese/North American communication at about the same time. Nishida began graduate work in communication at the University of Illinois, Chicago Circle, in the early 1970s. At about the same time, Gudykunst began working as an Intercultural Relations Specialist with the U.S. Navy in Yokosuka, Japan. We met when we began working on our doctorates at the University of Minnesota in 1975. While at Minnesota, we worked together facilitating Japanese/North American Intercultural Workshops and conducting training for North Americans going to Japan. After completing our doctorates, we began to conduct joint research on communication in Japan and the United States, as well as research on communication in Japanese/North American relationships. Most of our joint research has been published in English and Japanese (we cite the English publications in this book).

At the same time that we have been conducting joint research, Gudykunst has been developing a theory of effective interpersonal and intergroup communication (e.g., Gudykunst, 1988, 1993b). Gudykunst applied the theory to improving intergroup communication in *Bridging Differences* (Gudykunst, 1991, 1994), and Nishida led a group who translated this volume into Japanese. Our purpose in this volume is to integrate the cross-cultural research we have conducted with Gudykunst's theory to provide suggestions for how Japanese and North Americans can communicate more effectively with each other. We have drawn on the framework and material presented in *Bridging Differences* to accomplish this task and therefore have incorporated the title of the earlier book into the title of this volume.

Our approach to providing suggestions on improving communication effectiveness is more conceptual than that of other books on Japan and the United States. We believe it is important that you understand why Japanese and North American communication is similar or different if you are going to improve the quality of your communication. If you understand the principles outlined in this book, you should be able to make sense out of virtually any Japanese/North American encounter you might have. Our emphasis in this book is on helping North Americans communicate more effectively with Japanese. Although we are writing a separate book in Japanese to help Japanese communicate more effectively with North Americans, the information in this book should be useful to Japanese as well. If after reading this volume you want more details on communication in Japan and the United States, see Gudykunst (1993a).

Several people have contributed either directly or indirectly to our completion of the book. Bill Howell brought us together at Minnesota years ago. Harry Triandis' work on individualism-collectivism has had a major influence on our research, and Harry has commented on much of our work. Ellen Langer's work on mindfulness, Chuck Berger's work on uncertainty reduction, and Walter Stephan and Cookie Stephan's work on intergroup anxiety are incorporated into Gudykunst's theory. Michael Bond, Kwock Leung, Ge Gao, Karen Schmidt, Elizabeth Chua, Hiroko Koike Akasu, Nobuo Shiino, Seiichi Morisaki, Jiro Sakai, Georgette Wang, Robert Barraclough, Yoko Nadamitsu, Seung-Mock Yang, and Young-Chul Yoon collaborated on the research we have conducted. Yuko Matsumoto, Hiroshi Ota, Dan Bisgaard, and Stella Ting-Toomey provided suggestions on a draft of the book. The time to write the book was made available to the first author by a sabbatical leave from California State University, Fullerton.

—William B. Gudykunst
Laguna Beach, CA, USA

—Tsukasa Nishida
Shizuoka, Japan

1

Introduction

Prior to the Meiji Restoration, the Tokugawa Shoguns placed severe restrictions on contact between Japanese and *gaijin* (foreigners). Japanese who left Japan were forbidden from returning under penalty of death. There were, however, many contacts between Japanese and the outside world before Commodore Perry "opened" Japan to outside contact in 1853. Frequently ships sailing off the coast of Japan were caught in storms, and many were carried across the Pacific to North America. Japanese on these ships had contact with people in the United States, including Abraham Lincoln (Plummer, 1992). Many of these encounters were plagued by misunderstandings.

When Commodore Perry arrived in Japan, his sailors found the Japanese to be "the most polite people on earth" (cited by Dulles, 1965). Perry himself, however, reported that he was frustrated by the "lies" he was told and the "evasive" Japanese style of communication (Dulles, 1965). Dulles concluded that the opposing perceptions of Japanese courtesy and hypocrisy "helped set a pattern of American thinking about Japanese that has persisted for a century" (pp. 68-69). Virtually all accounts of the early contact indicate that cultural misunderstandings began with the first contact between people from Japan and the United States.

Many people believe that misunderstandings between Japanese and North Americans are due to one of the individuals not being competent in the other's language. Linguistic knowledge alone, however, is not enough to ensure that communication between Japanese and North Americans will progress smoothly or be effective. Confucius said that "human beings are drawn close to one another by their common nature, but habits and customs keep them apart." Misunderstandings between Japanese and North Americans often stem from not knowing the norms and rules guiding each other's communication. If, for example, North Americans can speak Japanese, but do not understand the Japanese culture, they can make fluent fools of themselves.

Language and culture are not the only factors that can contribute to misunderstandings between Japanese and North Americans. Attitudes (e.g., ethnocentrism) and stereotypes create expectations that often lead people to misinterpret each other's messages. People in Japan and the United States tend to have positive views of the other country. A *New York Times*, CBS News, and Tokyo Broadcasting System poll (conducted in November 1991; see Wiseman, 1991, for results), for example, indicates that 77% of the people in the United States "say their feelings toward Japan are generally friendly," and 65% of the people in Japan hold a similar sentiment toward the United States.[1] A *Time* (February 10, 1992) poll,[2] however, indicates that only 13% of the people in the United States think they know "a lot" about Japan and its people (42% think they know "some things") (Murrow, 1992); only 5% of the people in Japan think they know "a lot" about the United States and its people (42% think they know "some things") (Hillenbrand, 1992).

Even though North Americans and Japanese do not think they know a lot about the other culture, they hold complex stereotypes about each other. A *Time* (February 10, 1992) poll revealed that 94% of North Americans think that Japanese are competitive, 69% think they are crafty, 35% think they are devoted to fair play, 59% think they are friendly, 94% think they are hardworking, 4% think they are lazy, 12% think they are poorly educated, 53% think they are prejudiced, and 19% think they are violent

(Murrow, 1992). In contrast, 50% of the Japanese view people in the United States as competitive, 13% view them as crafty, 43% view them as devoted to fair play, 64% view them as friendly, 15% view them as hardworking, 21% view them as lazy, 21% view them as poorly educated, 41% view them as prejudiced, and 23% view them as violent (Hillenbrand, 1992). People in Japan admire the freedom of expression (89%), the variety of lifestyles (86%), the treatment of women (68%), and the leisure time available to workers (88%) in the United States (Hillenbrand, 1992). North Americans, on the other hand, admire Japanese industriousness (88%) and educational institutions (71%) (Murrow, 1992).

Improving understanding between people in the United States and Japan requires that cultural similarities and differences be recognized and negative stereotypes become more positive. Kitamura (1971) points out that "we have come to a stage in our [U.S.-Japan] relations in which we need hard understanding based on recognition and appreciation of differences rather than easy understanding based on similarities" (p. 37). Cultural similarities and differences are created and manifested through communication. It is impossible to improve relations between Japan and the United States without understanding how communication patterns are similar and different in the two cultures.

Improving communication between Japanese and North Americans requires that individuals become aware of how they communicate. Howell (1982) argues that awareness can be thought of as a four-stage process[3]: (1)"unconscious incompetence," where we misinterpret others' behavior, but are not aware of it; (2) "conscious incompetence," where we are aware that we misinterpret others' behavior, but do not do anything about it; (3) "conscious competence," where we think about our communication behavior and consciously modify it to improve our effectiveness (we refer to this stage as "mindfulness" below); and (4) "unconscious competence," where we have practiced the skills for effective communication to the extent that we no longer have to think about them to use them. Throughout the book, we point out areas where individuals may be unconsciously incompetent regarding Japanese/North

American communication and provide suggestions on how they can become consciously competent.

◆ Overview of Intercultural Communication

Everyone communicates and consider him- or herself to be an "expert" on the topic.[4] People think they know what the problems are and how to solve them. Unfortunately, many of the things taken for granted about communication lead to ineffective communication, especially when Japanese and North Americans are communicating. In this section, we overview the process of intercultural communication.

SYMBOLS, MESSAGES, AND MEANING

Language is a system of rules regarding how the sounds of the language are made, how sentences are formed, the meaning of words or combinations of words, and how the language is used. Language is a medium of communication. When the rules of language are translated into a channel of communication (e.g., the spoken word) using symbols, messages are created.

Symbols are things we use to represent something else. Virtually anything can be a symbol: words, nonverbal displays, flags, and so forth. Referents for symbols can include objects, ideas, or behaviors. There is no natural connection between a symbol and its referent. The relationship between a symbol and its referent is arbitrary and varies from culture to culture. Symbols are combined into messages, which are transmitted to others. Transmitting involves putting thoughts, feelings, emotions, and attitudes in a form recognizable by others. The messages created are transmitted to others who interpret them. Interpreting is the process of perceiving and making sense of the messages and other stimuli from the environment through the senses (seeing, hearing, touching, smelling, and tasting). How messages are transmitted and interpreted is influenced by individuals' cultural background and unique life experiences. The important point to keep in mind is that no two individuals have exactly the same life experiences. No two people, therefore, will transmit or interpret a message in the same way.

The term communication refers to the exchange of messages and the creation of meaning (e.g., assigning significance or interpreting the messages). Meanings cannot be transmitted from one person to another. Only messages can be transmitted. When a person transmits a message, he or she has a certain meaning in mind and then chooses the symbols and channel of communication accordingly. The person who interprets the message, however, attaches his or her own meaning to the message received. Messages are not transmitted and interpreted independently of one another. Both processes occur simultaneously. When a message is interpreted, the meaning attached to it is a function of the message itself, the channel used, the situation in which the message is interpreted, and the person who interprets it. Communication is effective to the extent that the person interpreting the message attaches a meaning to the message similar to what the transmitter intended (this idea is discussed in detail below).

There are two dimensions to any message: content and relationship dimensions (Watzlawick, Beavin, & Jackson, 1967). Content refers to the information in the message (e.g., what is said). The relationship component of a message is inferred from how the message is transmitted (including the specific words used), and it deals with how the participants are relating to each other. The way individuals communicate offers a definition of the relationship between them.

FUNCTIONS OF COMMUNICATION

There are many reasons why people communicate. They communicate to inform someone about something, to entertain another person, to change another person's attitudes or behavior, and to reinforce their view of themselves, to name only a few of the possibilities. It is impossible to examine all of the functions in a short book like this. We therefore focus on two specific functions that are related closely to effective intercultural communication between Japanese and North Americans: reducing uncertainty and reducing anxiety.[5]

Interacting with people from other cultures is a novel situation for most people in the United States and Japan. "The immediate psychological result of being in a new situation is lack of security. Ignorance of the potentialities inherent in the situation, of the means to reach a goal, and of the probable outcomes of an intended action causes insecurity" (Herman & Schield, 1961, p. 165). Attempts to deal with the ambiguity of new situations involves a pattern of information seeking (uncertainty reduction) and tension (anxiety) reduction (Ball-Rokeach, 1973).

The goal of information seeking and uncertainty reduction is understanding others. Three levels of understanding can be differentiated: description, prediction, and explanation (Berger et al., 1976). Description involves delineating what is observed in terms of its physical attributes (i.e., drawing a picture in words). Prediction involves projecting what will happen in a particular situation, and explanation involves stating why something occurred.

Individuals make predictions and create explanations whenever they communicate. They rarely describe others' behavior, however. When people communicate with others they typically interpret messages by attaching meaning to or making sense out of them. They do not stop to describe what they saw or heard before they interpret it. Rather, individuals interpret messages as they perceive them. The problem is that people base their interpretations on their culture and life experiences. Since one person's life experiences differ from another's, this often leads to misunderstandings.

Anxiety refers to the feeling of being uneasy, tense, worried, or apprehensive about what might happen. It is an affective (e.g., emotional) response, not a cognitive or behavioral response like uncertainty. Whereas uncertainty results from individuals' inability to predict others' behavior, "anxiety stems from the anticipation of negative consequences. People appear to fear at least four types of negative consequences: psychological or behavioral consequences for the self, and negative evaluations by members of the outgroup and the ingroup" (Stephan & Stephan, 1985, p. 159). Japanese and North Americans experience more uncertainty and anxiety when they communicate with members of the other culture than when they communicate with members of their own culture.

Individuals' ability to reduce uncertainty and manage anxiety influences the degree to which they can communicate effectively.[6] We do not mean to imply that Japanese and North Americans want to totally reduce their uncertainty and anxiety when they communicate with each other. Neither high nor low levels of uncertainty and anxiety are functional (Gudykunst, 1993). If anxiety is too high, people do not feel comfortable communicating with others. If anxiety is too low, they do not care enough to perform well. If uncertainty is too high, individuals cannot predict others' behavior. If uncertainty is too low, they get bored, or become overconfident in their predictions. Moderate levels of uncertainty and anxiety are desirable for communication effectiveness.

SOURCES OF COMMUNICATION BEHAVIOR

Communication behavior can be based on one of three sources.[7] First, communication behavior occurs out of habit. Japanese and North Americans have learned habits and scripts that they enact in particular situations. Scripts are predetermined courses of action. The greeting ritual is one example. The ritual for greeting others reduces the vast amount of uncertainty and anxiety present in initial interactions with strangers to manageable portions and allows people to interact with others as though there was relatively little uncertainty or anxiety. The norms and rules for the ritual provide predictions about how others will respond in the situation. When someone deviates from the script or a new situation is entered, people cannot fall back on the ritual's implicit predictions. Because greeting rituals differ across cultures, Japanese often deviate from

North American rituals and North Americans often deviate from Japanese rituals. When others do not conform to scripts, communicators must actively reduce their uncertainty before they can make accurate predictions and communicate effectively.

The second basis for communication behavior is intentions. Intentions are instructions individuals give themselves about how to communicate (Triandis, 1977). When people think about what they want to do in a particular situation, they form intentions. Intention, therefore, is a cognitive construct—it is part of one's thought processes. Japanese and North Americans' ability to accomplish their intentions when communicating with each other is a function, at least in part, of their motivation to communicate, knowledge of the other culture, and intercultural communication skills. We discuss these issues in detail in Chapter 6.

The final factor on which communication behavior may be based is affect, feelings, or emotions. People often react to others on a strictly emotional basis. If a person feels criticized, for example, he or she may become defensive and strike out at the other person without thinking. Individuals can, however, manage their emotional reactions cognitively. In fact, we argue below that this is necessary for effective communication to occur, especially when Japanese and North Americans communicate.

COMMUNICATIVE PREDICTIONS

"When people communicate they make predictions about the effects, or outcomes, of their communication behaviors; that is, they choose among various communicative strategies on the basis of predictions about how the person receiving the message will respond" (Miller & Steinberg, 1975, p. 7). Sometimes people are very conscious of the predictions they make and sometimes they are not. When Japanese and North Americans communicate, they also try to develop explanations for each other's behavior so they can understand why they communicate the way they do.

Miller and Steinberg (1975) isolate three different types of information used in making predictions about others: cultural, social, and personal.[8] People in any culture generally behave in a regular way because of the norms, rules, and values of their culture (we discuss culture in Chapter 2). This regularity allows cultural information to be used in making predictions. Miller and Sunnafrank (1982) point out that "knowledge about another person's culture—its language, beliefs, and prevailing ideology—often permits predictions of the person's probable response to messages. . . . Upon first encountering . . . [another person], cultural information provides the only grounds for communicative predictions" (p. 226).

Social predictions are based on memberships in or aspirations to particular social groups or social roles. Miller and Sunnafrank (1982) argue that social information is the principal kind of information used to predict behavior of people from the same culture. Group memberships based on ethnicity, company, gender, university, religion, disabilities, or gender orientation, for example, are used to predict others' behavior. Roles such as professor, physician, clerk, and supervisor also provide a basis for the sociological predictions we make.

When predictions are based on cultural or social information, an implicit assumption that the people within the category (e.g., the culture or ethnic group) are similar is made (Miller & Steinberg, 1975). Though individuals within a category share similarities (e.g., there are similarities among people born and raised in the United States), individuals within each of the categories also differ. When people are able to discriminate how individuals are similar to and different from other members of the same category, they are using personal information to make predictions. The use of personal information involves taking the specific person and how she or he will respond to messages into consideration when making predictions. The relative value placed on using personal and social information for making predictions is one of the major differences between the ways Japanese and North Americans communicate. To illustrate, North Americans emphasize personal information over social information in predicting others' behavior, whereas Japanese emphasize social information over personal information.

IDENTITY AND COMMUNICATION

Self-concept, how individuals define themselves, consists of three components: (1) personal identity, (2) social identity, and (3) human identity. Personal identity includes those aspects of a person's self-definition that makes him or her a unique individual. Personal identities are derived from unique individual experiences. Social identities, in contrast, are derived from shared memberships in social groups (including culture). Human identities are based on those characteristics shared with all humans.

Communication behavior can be based on our personal identities, our social identities, or both. In a particular situation, a person may choose (either consciously or unconsciously) to define her- or himself as unique person or as a member of a group. When communication behavior is based mostly on personal identities, interpersonal communication takes place. When people define themselves mostly in terms of their social identities (including cultural identities), in contrast, intergroup communication occurs. (Given this view, intercultural communication is a special case of intergroup communication, when cultural identity is guiding behavior.) Intergroup predictions are based on the category in which the other person is placed (e.g., member of my culture, not member of my culture). Social categorization refers to the way individuals order their social environment by grouping people in a way that makes sense to them (Tajfel, 1978). To illustrate, people can be divided into women and men, "Americans" and foreigners, or *Nihonjin* (Japanese) and *gaijin* (non-Japanese), to name only a few of the categories.

Once individuals place someone in a social category, their stereotype of people in that category is activated. Stereotypes are the mental pictures individuals have of a group of people. Stereotypes creates expectations about how people in the category will behave. When Japanese and North Americans communicate, the stereotypes that members of each culture have of their own culture and the other culture influence the predictions they make about each other. If people do not have clear stereotypes or have little knowledge of the other culture, they have no basis for making predictions. "This fact explains the uneasiness and perceived lack of control most people experience when thrust into an alien culture; they not only lack information about the individuals with whom they must communicate, they are bereft of information concerning shared cultural norms and values" (Miller & Sunnafrank, 1982, p. 227).

Personal *and* social identities influence all communication behavior, but one tends to predominate in a particular situation. When social identities have a greater influence on behavior than personal identities, however, there is an increased chance of misunderstandings occurring because individuals are likely to interpret each other's behavior based on their group memberships. In order to overcome the potential for misunderstandings that can occur when social identities predominate, communicators must acknowledge the cultural differences, as well as try to understand them and how they influence their communication. The remainder of the book is devoted to presenting information and skills that can be used to increase the accuracy of interpretations when Japanese and North Americans communicate. In the next section, we examine effective communication in more detail.

◆ Effective and Ineffective Communication

In the movie *Cool Hand Luke,* Paul Newman plays Luke, a man put in prison for destroying a parking meter. While in prison, Luke constantly gets into trouble with the prison staff. At one point when Luke had not done something that the warden asked him to do, the warden says to Luke, "What we have here is a failure to communicate." On the surface, the warden's statement makes sense. It is, however, incomplete. The warden and Luke communicated, but they did not communicate effectively.

WHY MISINTERPRETATIONS OCCUR

To say communication occurred does not imply an outcome. Communication is a process involving the exchange of messages and the creation of meaning. As indicated earlier, no two people ever attach exactly the same meaning to a message. Whether a specific instance of communication is effective depends on the degree to which the participants attach similar meanings to the messages exchanged. Powers and Lowrey (1984) refer to this as "basic communication fidelity"—"the degree of congruence between the cognitions [or thoughts] of two or more individuals following a communication event" (p. 58).

When individuals first encounter a new situation, they consciously seek cues to guide their behavior (Langer, 1978). As they have repeated experiences with the same event, they have less need to consciously think about their behavior. "The more often we engage in the activity, the more likely it is that we rely on scripts for the completion of the activity and the less likely there will be any correspondence between our actions and those thoughts of ours that occur simultaneously" (Langer, 1978, p. 39).

When people are engaging in habitual or scripted behavior, they are not highly aware of what they are doing or saying. To borrow an analogy from flying an airplane, they are on automatic pilot. In Langer's (1978) terminology, they are mindless. People do not communicate totally on automatic pilot; rather, they pay sufficient attention so that they can recall key words in conversations (Kitayama & Burnstein, 1988).

People communicating on automatic pilot interpret incoming messages based on the symbolic systems they learned as children. When Japanese and North Americans are communicating basing their interpretations on their own symbolic systems, ineffective communication is likely to occur. Misunderstandings can occur for a variety of reasons when Japanese and North Americans communicate. The message may not be transmitted in a way that can be understood, the message may be misinterpreted, or both can occur simultaneously. The problems that occur may also be due to pronunciation, grammar, familiarity with the topic being discussed, familiarity with the other person, familiarity with the other person's native language, fluency in the other person's language, or other social factors (Gass & Varonis, 1984). Generally speaking, the greater the cultural and linguistic knowledge, and the more cultural beliefs overlap with others, the less likelihood that there will be misunderstandings. Lack of linguistic and cultural knowledge contributes to misunderstandings because people "listen to speech, form a hypothesis about what routine is being enacted, and then rely on social background knowledge and co-occurrence expectations to evaluate what is intended and attitudes are conveyed" (Gumperz, 1982, p. 171).

To decrease the chance of misinterpretations of messages based on unconscious interpretations, individuals must be aware of their "normal" tendencies. Beck (1988) outlines five principles that are useful in understanding how misinterpretations occur:

1. We can never know the state of mind—the attitudes, thoughts, and feelings—of other people [especially people from other cultures].
2. We depend on signals, which are frequently ambiguous, to inform us about the attitudes and wishes of other people.
3. We use our own coding system [which is culturally based], which may be defective, to decipher these signals.
4. Depending on our own state of mind at a particular time, we may be biased in our method of interpreting other people's behavior. . . .
5. The degree to which we believe that we are correct in divining another person's motives and attitudes is not related to the actual accuracy of our belief. (p. 18)

Recognizing these principles can help improve the quality of communication. We apply the principles to Japanese/North American communication in Chapter 6.

MINDFULNESS

Individuals must become aware of their communication behavior in order to correct the tendency to misinterpret others' behavior and communicate more effectively. Social psychologists refer to this as becoming "mindful" of behavior. Langer (1989) isolates three qualities of mindfulness: "(1) creation of new categories; (2) openness to new information; and (3) awareness of more than one perspective" (p. 62). She points out that "categorizing is a fundamental and natural human activity. It is the way we come to know the world. Any attempt to eliminate bias by attempting to eliminate the perception of differences is doomed to failure" (p. 154).

Langer (1989) argues that what people need to do is learn to make more, not fewer, distinctions. To illustrate, North Americans who have only one broad category for Japanese can begin by dividing them into male and female. These categories can be further divided by age and whether the Japanese have been to the United States. The more subcategories used, the less North Americans' tendency to treat Japanese in a stereotypical fashion will be.

Openness to new information and awareness of more than one perspective are related to focusing on the process, rather than the outcome. Langer (1989) points out that

> an outcome orientation in social situations can induce mindlessness. If we think we know how to handle a situation, we don't feel a need to pay attention. If we respond to the situation as very familiar (as a result, for example, of overlearning), we notice only minimal cues necessary to carry out the proper scenarios. If, on the other hand, the situation is strange, we might be so preoccupied with the thought of failure ("what if I make a fool of myself?") that we miss nuances of our own and others' behavior. In this sense, we are mindless with respect to the immediate situation, although we may be thinking quite actively about outcome related issues. (p. 34)

Langer believes that focusing on the process (e.g., how individuals do something) forces individuals to be mindful of their behavior and pay attention to the situations in which they find themselves. It is only when individuals are mindful of the process of communication that they can determine how their interpretations of messages differ from others' interpretations of those messages.

Sometimes individuals become mindful of their communication without any effort because of the circumstances in which they find themselves. People tend to engage in habitual behavior and follow scripts only when they are available and nothing unusual to the scripts is encountered. There are, however, several factors that will cause individuals to become mindful of their communication: "(1) in novel situations where, by definition, no appropriate script exists, (2) where external factors prevent completion of a script, (3) when scripted behavior becomes effortful because substantially more of the behavior is required than is usual, (4) when a discrepant outcome is experienced, or (5) where multiple scripts come into conflict" (Berger & Douglas, 1982, pp. 46-47). Japanese and North Americans often are mindful of their behavior when they communicate with each other because the person from the other culture acts in a deviant or unexpected fashion, or because they do not have clear scripts to guide communication. The problem is that they usually are mindful of the outcome, not the process.

Because individuals tend to interpret others' behavior based on their own frame of reference, to communicate effectively with people from other cultures they need to become mindful of the process of communication, even when they are engaging in habitual behavior. We are not suggesting that people try to be mindful at all times. This would be impossible. Rather, we are suggesting that when individuals know there is a high potential for misunderstanding, they need to be mindful and consciously aware of the process of communication that is taking place.

◆ Plan for the Book

Our goal in this book is to explain similarities and differences in patterns of communication in Japan and the United States and to demonstrate how understanding these similarities and differences can help Japanese and North Americans communicate more effectively. Since this book is written in English, we emphasize explaining Japanese communication patterns for North Americans.[9] This should not, however, negate the usefulness of the book for Japanese.

The next three chapters focus on cross-cultural comparisons of selected aspects of communication in Japan and the United States. In Chapter 2, we examine similarities and differences in the cultures of Japan and the United States. Following this, we discuss how the Japanese and English languages influence communication in Chapter 3. In Chapter 4, we look at the major patterns of communication in Japan and the United States. The final two chapters focus on intercultural communication between Japanese and North Americans. We analyze how expectations influence Japanese/North American communication in Chapter 5. We conclude by providing suggestions for improving the quality of Japanese/North American communication in Chapter 6.

Notes

1. A Gallup poll conducted during the same time period, however, indicated that only 48% of the United States population hold a "favorable" attitude toward the Japanese. The differences may be due to wording of the questions. There also is rising "scorn" for the United States in Japan (see Helm, 1991). The figures have remained relatively constant over the years (see United States-Japan Advisory Commission, 1984, for figures in the 1970s and 1980s).

2. The poll was conducted in late January 1992 by Infoplan/Yankelovich International for *Time*.

3. Howell suggests a fifth stage, "conscious supercompetence," which is not included here.

4. Some of the ideas for this introduction were drawn from Fisher (1978).

5. These two functions are drawn from Gudykunst's (1988, 1993) theory of interpersonal and intergroup communication. He extended the work of Charles Berger and his associates (e.g., Berger & Bradac, 1982; Berger & Calabrese, 1975) on uncertainty reduction and Stephan and Stephan's (1985) work on anxiety.

6. A complete list of the factors contributing to the uncertainty and anxiety we experience can be found in the general version of the theory on which the book is based (Gudykunst, 1988, 1993).

7. The sources of behavior discussed below are based originally on the work of Triandis (1977). The specific discussion here is drawn from Gudykunst's extension of his work (Gudykunst, 1987; Gudykunst & Ting-Toomey, 1988).

8. They actually use the terms *sociological* and *psychological*.

9. We plan to write an equivalent volume for Japanese.

2

Cultural Similarities and Differences Between the United States and Japan

In order to communicate more effectively, we need to understand how the cultures of Japan and the United States are similar and different. Without understanding the nature of the two cultures, it is impossible to explain communication patterns in Japan and the United States. We begin by defining culture. Next we look at how cultures differ. Our focus is on isolating dimensions on which the United States and Japan can be compared (i.e., an etic analysis). This is necessary to explain cultural similarities and differences. We believe, however, that it also is important to incorporate cultural specific information to fully understand the two cultures. We conclude this chapter with a discussion of how cultural values influence communication.

◆ Culture

Keesing (1974) believes that culture is a person's

theory of what his [or her] fellows know, believe, and mean, his [or her] theory of the code being followed, the game being played,

17

in the society into which he [or she] was born. . . . It is this theory
to which a native actor [or actress] refers in interpreting the unfa-
miliar or the ambiguous, in interacting with [others]. (p. 89)

Keesing goes on to point out that individuals' understanding of
their culture is mainly unconscious. That is, they are not highly
aware of how their culture influences their behavior. When
individuals communicate on automatic pilot, they follow rules,
but they are not highly aware of the rules being followed. Keesing
also points out that no two individuals share the same theory
of their culture, but there is sufficient overlap in how members
of a culture view their culture so that they can communicate with
each other. "Culture in this view is ordered not simply as a col-
lection of symbols fitted together by the analyst but as a system
of knowledge, shaped and constrained by the way the human
brain acquires, organizes, and processes information and creates 'internal models of reality'" (Keesing, 1974, p. 89). To use
Hofstede's (1991) metaphor, our culture is the "software of our
mind."

Keesing's definition of culture suggests that it is individuals'
theory of the "game being played" when interacting with others.
Culture provides guidelines for how individuals should interact
with others and how they should interpret others' behavior.
Culture, therefore, provides a system of knowledge for dealing
with the world. We use the term culture to refer to the "system
of knowledge" that is shared by a large group of people. The
borders between cultures usually, but not always, coincide with
political boundaries between countries. To illustrate, we can
talk about the culture of the United States and the Japanese
culture. It is important to recognize, however, that there are
individual variations in the ways that people understand their
culture. Though members of a culture share a large part of their
culture, each person has a unique view of his or her culture.

It is recognized widely that the United States is a very diverse
culture. Most North Americans, however, tend to see Japan as
highly homogeneous. This is not actually the case. Miyanaga
(1991) points out that there can be

antagonism between those from the eastern and western regions of Japan; those from the west often complain that they never feel accepted in Tokyo, located in the east. In western Japan, people from the east are referred to as *bando mono*, literally "a person from the east," which carries a derogatory connotation of "uncivilized." In the same way that ethnic background carries associative connotations in [North] America, regional (prefectural) backgrounds are socially significant to the Japanese. (p. 12)

Miyanaga also indicates that all Japanese speak two versions of Japanese: standardized and their own dialect or accent. Standard Japanese is spoken in social situations, but individuals use their own dialect or accent in their local region and with members of their ingroups.

◆ How Cultures Differ

In order to understand similarities and differences in communication across cultures, it is necessary to have a way of talking about how cultures differ. It does not make any sense to say that "Yuko communicates indirectly because she is a Japanese" or that "Robin communicates directly because she is from the United States." This does not tell us why there are differences between the way people communicate in the United States and Japan. There has to be some aspect of the cultures in Japan and the United States that is different, and this difference, in turn, explains why Japanese communicate indirectly and people from the United States communicate directly. In other words, there are variables on which cultures can be different or similar that can be used to explain communication across cultures. We refer to these variables as "dimensions of cultural variability."[1] We focus on those that we have found useful in understanding similarities and differences in Japan and the United States: individualism-collectivism, low- and high-context communication, uncertainty avoidance, power distance, and masculinity-femininity.[2]

INDIVIDUALISM-COLLECTIVISM

Individualism-collectivism is the major dimension of cultural variability used to explain cross-cultural differences in behavior.[3] Emphasis is placed on individuals' goals in individualistic cultures, whereas group goals have precedence over individuals' goals in collectivistic cultures. Individualistic cultures like the United States, for example, promote self-realization:

> Chief among the virtues claimed by individualist philosophers is self-realization. Each person is viewed as having a unique set of talents and potentials. The translation of these potentials into actuality is considered the highest purpose to which one can devote one's life. The striving for self-realization is accompanied by a subjective sense of rightness and personal well-being. (Waterman, 1984, pp. 4-5)

Self-realization often is viewed as the primary goal in individualistic cultures (e.g., Maslow's, 1971, hierarchy of needs places self-actualization as the highest human need).

Collectivistic cultures require that individuals fit into the group. In collectivistic cultures individuals define themselves by referring to their relations to others. Lebra (1976), for example, points out that

> the Japanese concern for belonging relates to the tendency toward collectivism, which is expressed by an individual's identification with the collective goal of the group to which he [or she] belongs. Collectivism thus involves cooperation and solidarity, and the sentimental desire for the warm feeling of *ittaikan* ("feeling oneness") with fellow members of one's group is widely shared by Japanese. (p. 25)

Group membership is stressed by many writers on Japanese culture (e.g., Nakane, 1970; see Zander, 1983, for a discussion of the importance placed on group membership in Japan).

To fully understand how individualism and collectivism are manifested in Japan and the United States, it is necessary to look at several specific issues. The two general areas that differentiate the two cultures involve the predominant self-construals and the role of the ingroup. Furthermore, several Japanese concepts (*wa*, *amae*, and *enryo*) that are manifestations of the specific form that collectivism takes in Japan need to be discussed.

Self-Conceptions

An independent self-construal predominates in individualistic cultures, whereas an interdependent self-construal predominates in collectivistic cultures.[4] An independent self-construal involves seeing oneself as a separate, unique person whose self-definition does not include others. An interdependent self-construal, in contrast, involves defining oneself in relation to others.

Hamaguchi (1983) summarizes the ways individuals view themselves in Japan and the United States. In the United States, an "individual

> holds a conviction that he [or she] is a firmly established substance which is solely independent, and, therefore, cannot be invalidated by others. Also, he [or she] is convinced that he [or she] is the master of himself [or herself], but at the same time he [or she] is liable for his [or her] own deeds. The individual objectifies such an assertion (that he [or she] is undoubtedly himself [or herself]) and the sense of autonomy. (pp. 140-141)

Japanese, in contrast, view themselves contextually:

> For the Japanese, "self" means the portion which is distributed to him [or her], according to the situation he [or she] is in, from the living space shared between himself [or herself] and the other person with whom he [or she] had developed a mutually dependent relationship.
>
> A reason why this self-consciousness of the Japanese is formed this way is probably that self and others are in a symbiotic relationship, and that they believe that their beings depend largely on other beings. . . . This relativistic "self" can easily be mistaken for being unindependent. . . . However, here, selves are "mutually dependent," and their spontaneous fulfillment of the needs are intentionally controlled. (p. 142)

Similar differences in the way Japanese and North Americans view themselves are isolated by other writers (e.g., Markus & Kitayama, 1991).

Ingroups

Triandis (1988) argues that collectivistic cultures emphasize goals, needs, and views of the ingroup over those of the individual; the social norms of the ingroup rather than individual pleasure; shared ingroup beliefs rather than unique individual beliefs; and a value on cooperation with ingroup members rather than maximizing individual outcomes. In individualistic cultures, "people are supposed to look after themselves and their immediate family only," whereas in collectivistic cultures, "people belong to ingroups or collectivities which are supposed to look after them in exchange for loyalty" (Hofstede & Bond, 1984, p. 419).

The boundary between an ingroup and outgroup is very important in Japan. It is related to the general tendency to draw a boundary between inside and outside in various situations. Lebra (1976), for example, points out that

> the Japanese are known to differentiate their behavior by whether the situation is defined as *uti* or *soto*. . . . Where the demarcation line is drawn varies widely: it may be inside versus outside an individual person, a family, a group of playmates, a school, a company, a village, or a nation. It is suggestive that the term *uti* is used colloquially to refer to one's house, family, or family member, and the shop or company where one works. (p. 112)

Who is an insider and who is an outsider, then, depends on the situation and the individuals communicating.

The number of ingroups, the extent of influence for each ingroup, and the depth of the influence must be taken into consideration in the analysis of individualism-collectivism (Triandis, 1988). Because individualistic cultures have many specific ingroups, they exert less influence on individuals than ingroups do in collectivistic cultures. There are only a few general in-groups (e.g., work group, university, family) in collectivistic cultures, so they have a large influence on behavior. Although the ingroup may be the same in individualistic and collectivistic cultures, the sphere of its influence is different. The sphere of influence in an individualistic culture is very specific (e.g., the ingroup affects behavior in very specific circumstances), where-as the sphere of influence in a collectivistic culture is very general (e.g., the ingroup affects behavior in many different aspects of a person's life).

Ingroups have different rank orders of importance in collec-tivistic cultures; some, for example, put family ahead of all other ingroups, whereas others put their companies ahead of other in-groups (Triandis, 1988). Nakane (1970), for example, points out that

> when a Japanese "faces the outside" (confronts another person) and affixes some position to himself [or herself] socially he [or she] is inclined to give precedence to institution over kind of occupa-tion. . . . In group identification, a frame such as a "company" or "association" is of primary importance; the attribute of the individ-ual is a secondary matter. (p. 2)

If the person is a college student or faculty member, the in-stitution with which he or she will identify is the university. Students' identification with the university continues even after they graduate.

The Japanese Concept of Wa

Virtually all writers on Japanese culture indicate that *wa* is a central value. Like many Japanese words, however, there is no direct equivalent for *wa* in English.[5] *Wa* often is translated as harmony, but this does not capture the complete essence of the concept. The importance of *wa* can be traced back to Prince Shootoku and the first article of the constitution written in the seventh century: "Above all else esteem concord" (Nakamura,

1968, p. 633). "Concord" is the word used for *wa*. As indicated earlier, concord or harmony alone is not sufficient to understand *wa*. To better understand the concept, consider how Kawashima (1967) contrasts the role of *wa* in Japan with individualism:

> In individualism there can exist co-operation, compromise, self-sacrifice, and so on, in order to adjust and reduce contradictions and oppositions, but in the final analysis there exists no real harmony (*wa*) . . . the *wa* of [Japan] is not mechanical co-operation, starting from reason, of equal individuals independent of each other, but the grand harmony (*taiwa*) which maintains its integrity by proper statuses of individuals within the collectivity by acts in accordance with these statuses. (p. 264)

He goes on to point out that when divergent viewpoints are integrated into a unity, then *wa* emerges.

Kawashima's description also suggests that harmony clearly is linked to a collectivity or group, specifically the ingroup. The value placed on *wa* does not extend to relations between ingroups and outgroups. De Vos (1985), for example, points out that *wa* within an ingroup can create competition with members of other groups.

Wierzbica (1991) points out that *wa* is something that "is desired or aimed for" in Japanese groups. Wierzbica contends that this explains why *wa* is so frequently used as a slogan or motto in Japan by companies and people responsible for the success of different groups (e.g., baseball coaches). She points out that *wa* generally is not discussed in conjunction with naturally cohesive groups like the family.[6]

Wa is possible, in part, because Japanese draw a clear distinction between *tatemae* and *honne*. *Tatemae* refers to the principle or standard by which a person is bound, at least outwardly (it is a public presentation). *Honne*, in contrast, refers to a person's "real" or inner wishes (Lebra, 1976). *Wa* is developed and maintained through *tatemae*, not *honne*. We discuss this issue in more detail below.

The Japanese Concept of Amae.

The interdependence derived from the Japanese form of collectivism is linked directly to the importance of *amae*.[7] *Amae* often is translated as "dependence." Wierzbica (1991) points out, however, that "dependence" does not capture the pragmatic meaning of *amae*.

Doi (1973) defines *amae* as "the noun form of *amaeru*, an intransitive verb which means 'to depend and presume upon another's benevolence.' . . . [It involves] helplessness and the desire to be loved" (p. 22). He contends that *amae* is "a thread that runs through all of the various activities in Japanese society" (p. 26).

Doi argues that *amae* is based on infants' relationships with their mothers. Although *amae* is not limited to family relationships, when it occurs in other relationships it is perceived in terms of the relationship between a parent and a child. *Amae* involves a "trustful dependence" that nothing bad will happen if one person is dependent upon another person who has good feelings for him or her. Doi also points out that *amae* involves conscious awareness; that is, Japanese are consciously aware of those upon whom they depend.[8]

The Japanese Concept of Enryo

Enryo often is translated as "reserve" or "restraint." Lebra (1976) points out that *enryo* is a response to group pressure for conformity. In the presence of this pressure Japanese may refrain from expressing opinions that go against the majority. Wierzbica (1991) contends that *enryo* is not limited to personal opinions; it also involves restraint from expressing desires, wishes, or preferences. Further, it includes sidestepping choices when they are offered (Smith, 1983). This extends to declining to state what is convenient or even desired when asked (Mizutani & Mizutani, 1987).

Lebra (1976) clearly links *enryo* to collectivism in Japan. She points out that it is a product of the suppression of individuality under the pressure of group solidarity and conformity, empathetic considerations for [others'] convenience or comfort, concern to prevent our [own] embarrassment, and the wish to maintain [our] freedom by avoiding social involvement without hurting [others]. (p. 252)

Wierzbica (1991) believes that *enryo* is a conscious or semiconscious attitude and that it is expressed verbally and nonverbally to others.

Variation Within Cultures

Most scholars agree that the United States is an individualistic culture and Japan is a collectivistic culture (Hofstede's [1980] scores for the United States [91] and Japan [46] support this conclusion).[9] Although these terms are not heavily value laden in the United States, the translations of both terms are value laden in Japan. Ito (1989b), for example, points out that Japanese scholars do not use the translation of the term collectivism, *zentaishugi*, because it often is used to refer to dictatorial political systems. Rather, they use terms like "group oriented" (*shudanshugi*; Nakane, 1970, among others), "relationalism" (*aidagarashugi*; Kumon, 1982), "contextualism" (*kanjinshugi*; Hamaguchi, 1982), or "interindividualism" (*saijinshugi*; Ito, 1989a). Ito (1989b) also points out that the term used for "individualism" in Japanese, *kojinshugi*, also has negative connotations (e.g., selfishness).

Critiques of the *nihonjinron* (literally, discussion of the Japanese) approach or the group model of Japanese society (e.g., Befu, 1980a, 1980b) suggest that blind acceptance of this model, with its emphasis on harmony and *giri* (voluntary feelings of obligation, discussed in more detail below), leads scholars to overlook Japanese "personhood" (e.g., concepts such as *seishin* or *jinkaku*).[10] Befu, for example, argues that *seishin* deals with "individuals qua individuals." "*Seishin* has to do with one's spiritual disposition, one's inner strength, which results from character building and self-discipline" (Befu, 1980b, pp. 180-181;

see Rohlen, 1973, for a discussion of this concept). He further suggests that "behind the appearance of group solidarity one will find each member is being motivated more by personal ambitions than by his [or her] blind loyalty to the group. Put another way, Japanese are loyal to their groups because it pays to be loyal" (Befu, 1977, p. 87).

Befu (1980b) contends that the concepts of *tatemae* and *honne* must be considered in explaining personhood in Japan. Yoneyama (1973) also argues that the distinction between public matters (*oyake-goto*) and private matters (*watakushi-goto*) must always be taken into consideration when analyzing Japanese communication (see also Doi's [1986] discussion of *omote* and *ura*). Befu (1980a, 1980b) contends that the group model can explain public matters, but not private matters. This contention is supported by two studies of value orientations in Japan. Caudill and Scarr (1961) and Nishida (1981) found that although collaterality predominates in Japan, the value orientation (collaterality, lineality, individualism) that individuals select depends on the specific sphere of life being examined.

Before proceeding, it also should be noted that focusing only on the individualistic tendencies in the United States leads scholars to overlook collectivistic aspects of the culture (for a recent discussion see Bellah, Madsen, Sullivan, Swidler, & Tipton, 1985; Wuthnow, 1991). Kluckhohn and Strodtbeck (1961), for example, point out that although individualism predominates in the United States, collaterality and lineality (two forms of collectivism) also affect behavior. Nishida (1981) found that although individualism predominates overall in the United States, the value orientation (individualism, collaterality, lineality) that individuals select depends on the specific sphere of life being examined.

LOW- AND HIGH-CONTEXT COMMUNICATION

Individualism-collectivism provides a powerful explanatory framework for understanding cultural similarities and differences of communication in multinational corporations. Whereas individualism-collectivism defines broad differences between cultures, Hall's (1976) low- and high-context scheme focuses upon cultural differences in communication processes.

Hall (1976) differentiates cultures on the basis of the communication that predominates in the culture. A high-context communication or message is one in which "most of the information is either in the physical context or internalized in the person, while very little is in the coded, explicit, transmitted part of the message" (Hall, 1976, p. 79). A low-context communication or message, in contrast, is one in which "the mass of information is vested in the explicit code" (p. 70). Although no culture exists at either end of the continuum, the culture of the United States is placed toward the lower end, slightly above the German, Scandinavian, and Swiss cultures. Most Asian cultures, such as the Japanese, Chinese, and Korean, in contrast, fall toward the high-context end of the continuum.

The level of context influences all other aspects of communication:

> High-context cultures make greater distinction between insiders and outsiders than low-context cultures do. People raised in high-context systems expect more of others than do the participants in low-context systems. When talking about something that they have on their minds, a high-context individual will expect his [or her] interlocutor to know what's bothering him [or her], so that he [or she] doesn't have to be specific. The result is that he [or she] will talk around and around the point, in effect putting all the pieces in place except the crucial one. Placing it properly—this keystone—is the role of his [or her] interlocutor. (Hall, 1976, p. 98)

It appears that low- and high-context communication are the predominant forms of communication in individualistic and collectivistic cultures, respectively (Gudykunst & Ting-Toomey, 1988).

As suggested earlier, members of low-context, individualistic cultures tend to communicate in a direct fashion, whereas members of high-context, collectivistic cultures tend to communicate in an indirect fashion. Levine (1985) describes communication in the United States (an individualistic culture) as leaving "little room for the cultivation of ambiguity. The dominant [North] American temper calls for clear and direct communication. It expresses itself in such common injunctions as 'Say what you mean,' 'Don't beat around the bush,' and 'Get to the point'" (p. 28). Similarly, Okabe (1983) points out that

> [North] Americans' tendency to use explicit words is the most noteworthy characteristic of their communicative style. They prefer to employ such categorical words as "absolutely," "certainty," and "positively." . . . The English syntax dictates that the absolute "I" be placed at the beginning of a sentence in most cases, and that the subject-predicate relation be constructed in an ordinary sentence. (p. 36)

Communicators in the United States, therefore, emphasize direct, low-context communication.

In describing communication in Japan, Okabe (1983) suggests that the collectivistic

> cultural assumptions of interdependence and harmony require that Japanese speakers limit themselves to implicit and even ambiguous use of words. In order to avoid leaving an assertive impression, they like to depend . . . on qualifiers such as "maybe," "perhaps," "probably," and "somewhat." Since Japanese syntax does not require the use of a subject in a sentence, the qualifier-predicate is a predominate form of sentence construction. (p. 36)

Many other writers make similar observations (e.g., Johnson & Johnson, 1975). Children in Japan are taught not to call attention to themselves or take the initiative verbally. Rather, they are taught to foster *enryo*, ritualized verbal self-depreciation used to maintain group harmony.

There are two Japanese concepts that are related closely to Hall's notion of low- and high-context messages. Mushakoji (1976) contends that an *erabi* view of the world involves constructing messages with the idea of persuading others. The *awase* view of the world, in contrast, involves a speaker's adjusting to the people listening. Mushakoji points out that *awase* logic does not depend upon standardized word meanings. Expressions have multifarious nuances and are considered to be only signals which hint at reality rather than describing it precisely. Words are not taken at face value; it is necessary to infer the meaning behind them. In contrast to *erabi* culture in which the face value of words is trusted most and one is expected to act on it, in *awase* society it is possible to "hear one and understand ten." It is interesting to note that in Japan it is considered virtuous to "catch on quickly" (*sasshi ga hayai*), in other words, to adjust to someone's position before it is logically and clearly enunciated. (p. 43)

Erabi logic is related closely to low-context communication, whereas *awase* logic is related closely to high-context communication.

To summarize, low-context communication can be characterized as being direct, univocal, absolute, with a focus on the speaker. High-context communication, in contrast, can be characterized as indirect, ambiguous, qualified, and with a focus on the receiver. Low- and high-context communication patterns exist in all cultures, but one tends to predominate.[11] We examine how direct and indirect forms of communication are manifested in language usage in the next chapter.

UNCERTAINTY AVOIDANCE

In comparison to members of cultures low in uncertainty avoidance, members of cultures high in uncertainty avoidance have a lower tolerance "for uncertainty and ambiguity, which expresses itself in higher levels of anxiety and energy release, greater need for formal rules and absolute truth, and less tolerance for people or groups with deviant ideas or behavior" (Hofstede, 1979, p. 395). In high uncertainty avoidance cultures, aggressive behavior of self and others is acceptable; however, individuals prefer to contain aggression by avoiding conflict and competition. There is a strong desire for consensus in cultures high in uncertainty avoidance, and therefore deviant behavior is not acceptable. Members of high uncertainty avoidance cultures also tend to display emotions more than members of low uncertainty avoidance cultures. People in low uncertainty avoidance cultures have lower stress levels and weaker superegos, and they accept dissent and take risks more than people in high uncertainty avoidance cultures.

Hofstede (1991) points out that uncertainty avoidance should not be equated with risk avoidance. He goes on to point out that people in

> uncertainty avoiding cultures shun ambiguous situations. People in such cultures look for a structure in their organizations, institutions, and relationships which makes events clearly interpretable and predictable. Paradoxically, they are often prepared to engage in risky behavior to reduce ambiguities, like starting a fight with a potential opponent rather than sitting back and waiting. (p. 116)

Hofstede summarizes the view of people in high uncertainty avoidance cultures as "what is different, is dangerous," (p. 119) and the credo of people in low uncertainty avoidance cultures as "what is different, is curious" (p. 119).

Uncertainty avoidance is useful in understanding differences in how strangers are treated. People in high uncertainty avoidance cultures try to avoid ambiguity. They therefore develop rules and rituals for virtually every possible situation in which they might find themselves, including interacting with strangers. Interaction with strangers in cultures high in uncertainty avoidance may be highly ritualistic and very polite. If people from high uncertainty avoidance cultures interact with strangers in a situation where there are not clear rules, they may ignore the strangers—treat them as though they do not exist. By ignoring strangers in these situations, members of high uncertainty avoidance cultures are able to avoid the ambiguity and stress inherent in the situation.

As with individualism-collectivism, both low and high degrees of uncertainty avoidance exist in every culture, but one tends to predominate. Given Hofstede's (1980) scores for uncertainty avoidance, Japan (92) is classified as a high uncertainty avoidance culture and the United States (46) is considered a low uncertainty avoidance culture.

One indication of the validity of these scores is the importance of rules in Japan. Edgerton (1985), for example, points out that outsiders often view Japan as "regimented," "rigid," "closely ordered," and "oppressively controlled." He argues that in Japan "one gained virtue by following the rules and lost it by failing to do so" (p. 176). Edgerton goes on to suggest that "there are legitimate exceptions to rules in Japan today based on age, gender, intoxication, ceremony, and various settings. These exceptions are as clearly understood as the rules that they exempt one from following" (p. 177).

POWER DISTANCE

Power distance is defined as "the extent to which the less powerful members of institutions and organizations accept that power is distributed unequally" (Hofstede & Bond, 1984, p. 419). Individuals from high power distance cultures accept power as part of society: superiors consider their subordinates to be different from themselves and vice versa. People in low power distance cultures, in contrast, see superiors and subordinates as the same kinds of people, with differences in power being due to the roles they are filling. Outside the role, superiors and subordinates are equal in low power distance cultures.

People in high power distance cultures see power as a basic fact in society and stress coercive or referent power, whereas people in low power distance cultures believe power should be used only when it is legitimate and prefer to use expert or legitimate power (Hofstede, 1980). Hofstede (1991) also points out that

> in small power distance countries there is limited dependence of subordinates on bosses, and a preference for consultation, that is, *interdependence* between boss and subordinate. The emotional distance between them is relatively small: subordinates will quite readily approach and contradict their bosses. In large

power distance countries there is considerable dependence of subordinates on bosses. Subordinates respond by either *preferring* such dependence (in the form of an autocratic or paternalistic boss), or rejecting it entirely, which in psychology is known as *counterdependence*: that is dependence, but with a negative sign. (p. 27)

The power distance dimension clearly influences the relationship between superiors and subordinates in organizations.

Power distance is useful in understanding behavior in role relationships, particularly those involving different degrees of power or authority. People from high power distance cultures, for example, do not question their superiors' orders. They expect to be told what to do. People in low power distance cultures, in contrast, do not necessarily accept superiors' orders at face value; they want to know why they should follow them. When people from the two different systems interact, misunderstanding is likely unless one or both understand the other person's system.

Low and high power distance tendencies exist in all cultures, but one tends to predominate. Based on Hofstede's (1980) scores, Japan (54) and the United States (40) are relatively similar on this dimension. Hofstede's scores, however, may not be an accurate reflection of where Japan and the United States fall on this dimension. Nakane (1970), for example, points out that in Japan "if we postulate a social group embracing members with various different attributes, the method of tying together the constituent members will be based on the vertical relation" (p. 24). Nakane argues that in Japan the vertical relation provides the basis for group cohesion and that "even a set of individuals sharing identical qualifications tend to create *difference* among these individuals" (p. 26). The major factors on which vertical relations are formed include age, position, experience, and knowledge (Midooka, 1990). Gender is also a characteristic on which vertical relationships are formed. It is also important to recognize that age may cut across other vertical relationships. To illustrate, a person of higher status may use polite language to a person of lower status who is older. In contrast to Japan, the

United States is considered as being arranged on horizontal relationships. We discuss how these differences are reflected in language usage in the next chapter.

Two Japanese concepts related to vertical relationships need to be mentioned, *on* and *giri*. *On* involves one person's doing a favor for another, with the result that the person for whom the favor was done owes a debt to the person who did the favor (Lebra, 1974). Lebra (1974) points out that "an *on* must be accepted with gratitude since it is evidence of a giver's benevolence or generosity; at the same time it must be carried as a burden, because the *on*, once granted, makes the receiver a debtor and compels him [or her] to repay" (p. 194). Most writers contend that *on* imposes an obligation on the person receiving the favor and suggest that *on* occurs in vertical relationships.

Lebra (1976) indicates that the person receiving the *on* does not externally demonstrate gratitude to the person granting the favor, but rather maintains an awareness of being in debt to and recognizing the person granting the favor as a benefactor. Not all debts, however, create *on*, only those that are perceived to be "unpayable" (Wierzbica, 1991). Lebra (1974) contends that the relationship between the individuals involved is "asymmetrical in that the *on* is considered limitless and unpayable and that the receiver feels urged to return at least 'one-ten-thousandth' of the received sum through total, sometimes life-long, devotion to the donor" (p. 195).

Giri often is defined as duty or obligation. These definitions do not, however, provide a complete understanding of its pragmatic meaning.[12] *Giri* clearly involves a sense of obligation, but it is an obligation to a particular person with whom one interacts. Although *on* also involves obligation, it can be an obligation to a category of people such as ancestors, the emperor, or the country. Lebra (1976) indicates that *giri* encompasses all aspects of a person's life. *Giri* is "a moral imperative to perform one's duties toward other members of one's group" (Befu, 1986, p. 162). It provides a special bond between individuals and can strengthen existing relationships that are viewed as more or less permanent (Wierzbica, 1991).

Giri may be based on a particular relationship between individuals or it might arise because of a favor one person does for another. Dore (1958) points out that

> *giri*-relationships may be "ascribed" in the sense that they are implied in the very nature of the position occupied by two parties . . . relations between relatives not of the same household group, relations between employer and employee, between landlord and tenant, between neighbors, or between fellow-employees. They may also arise as the result of a particular favor conferred, for example, relations between marriage go-between and married pair, or between employee and the [person] who found [the] job. (p. 254)

A person who violates the obligations in a *giri* relationship will be labeled as lacking integrity or honor (Smith, 1983).

MASCULINITY-FEMININITY

Members of cultures high in masculinity value things, power, and assertiveness, whereas members of cultures low in masculinity (or high in femininity) value people, quality of life, and nurturance (Hofstede, 1980). Cultures high in masculinity emphasize differentiated sex roles and performance. Conversely, cultures low in masculinity emphasize fluid sex roles and quality of life.

Masculinity-femininity is useful in understanding cultural differences and similarities in opposite-sex and same-sex relationships. People from highly masculine cultures, for example, tend to have little contact with members of the opposite sex when they are growing up. They tend to see same-sex relationships as more intimate than opposite-sex relationships. For people from a feminine culture to communicate effectively with strangers from a masculine culture, especially if they are male and female, they must understand the others' orientation toward sex roles.

As with the other dimensions of cultural variability, both masculinity and femininity tendencies exist in all cultures. One tendency, however, tends to predominate. Based on Hofstede's (1980) scores, Japan (95) is viewed as a highly masculine culture, whereas the United States (62) is a low masculine culture (but not a feminine culture).

White's (1993) research on teenagers in Japan and the United States supports the distinction between Japan and the United States drawn here. She points out that Japanese teenagers form three types of relationships: (1) best friends (*shinyuu*) who provide intimate relationships (a typical student will have two or three best friends), (2) group friends who " provide standards for peer acceptance, a testing ground for the tensions between a newly emerging sense of self and the demands of the group" (p. 142; a group is an even number, usually six or eight), and (3) *sempai-kohai* (senior-junior) relationships, which occur in formal and informal student clubs. White contends that both best friends and group friends are members of the same sex. She points out the group friends spend so much time together that it is difficult for either boys or girls to spend time with members of the opposite sex. "When a girl actually does go steady, she may be seen as remote, even unavailable, to her friends, who feel betrayed" (p. 155). Teenagers in the United States, in contrast, do not experience the same pressure to interact with members of the same sex, and they develop friendships with members of the opposite sex.[13]

Notes

1. Our approach to discussing similarities and differences between Japan and the United States, therefore, is etic in nature. We use emic analyses to explain how the etic dimensions are manifested in Japan and the United States. Japanese writers using a *Nihonjinron* approach to the study of Japanese culture argue that an etic approach does not yield accurate descriptions of Japanese culture (see Dale, 1986, for examples). Hamaguchi (1983), for example, argues that collectivism is not an accurate description of Japanese culture. His contextualism, however, sounds very similar to collectivism and is similar to the interdependent self-construal that Markus and Kitayama (1991) describe. We believe that etic analyses are necessary when the goal is to compare and

contrast cultures (which is our purpose here), but emic analyses also are necessary to completely understand any culture.

2. Hofstede (1980) isolated four dimensions: individualism, uncertainty avoidance, power distance, and masculinity. The Chinese Culture Connection (1987) isolated a fifth, Confucian work dynamism. This dimension has not been clearly linked to communication even though Yum (1988) tries to link Confucianism to communication. She does not, however, clearly differentiate Confucianism and collectivism.

3. It should be noted that this dimension is isolated not only by theorists in "Western" cultures, but also by theorists from "Eastern" cultures (see Chinese Culture Connection, 1987, for an example).

4. See Markus and Kitayama (1991) for a complete discussion of independent and interdependent self-construals. See also Rosenberger (1992) for recent discussions of the Japanese self.

5. See Wierzbica (1991) for an attempt to define several Japanese key words (*amae, enryo, wa, on, giri*, and *seishin*) and how they are related to Japanese core values.

6. The family structure in Japan is becoming more "loose" over time, and this claim may not apply to all families.

7. Murase (1984) argues that Japan is a *sunao* culture that is relationship oriented. This orientation leads to personality characteristics that emphasize dependency (*amae*).

8. See Fujihara and Kurokawa (1981) for a scale to measure *amae* in Japan.

9. The only difference to emerge in the study by Triandis, Bontempo, Villareal, Asai, and Lucca (1988) is that Japanese students are more likely than students in the United States to report that they would pay attention to the views of their co-workers. Triandis et al. conclude that "the Japanese feel honored when their ingroups are honored and pay attention to the views of some, but not all, ingroups; they subordinate their goals to the goals of some ingroups" (p. 333). One problem with this study is that the researchers did not take into consideration the degree to which the respondents identified with their culture. Gudykunst, Nishida, Chung, and Sudweeks (1992) found that strength of cultural identity and perceived typicality influence the individualistic and collectivistic values that students in Japan and the United States hold. Yamaguchi (1990) found that collectivism among Japanese is associated positively with sensitivity to rejection, affiliative tendency, and self-monitoring, whereas it is associated negatively with need for uniqueness and internal locus of control. For a recent discussion of how individualism-collectivism is manifested in elementary school classrooms, see Hamilton, Blumenfeld, Akoh, and Miura (1991).

10. See Nakamura (1967) for an earlier discussion of the individual in Japanese society. See Ito (1989b) for a review of Japanese views on interpersonal communication; see Midooka (1990) for a recent discussion of Japanese styles of communication.

11. Low- and high-context messages are similar to Bernstein's (1973) distinction between elaborated and restricted codes, respectively.

12. See Minamoto (1969) and Nishida and Nishida (1978) for discussions of *giri*.

13. It also should be noted that relationships in Japan tend to be long term. Relationships established in high school, and college, for example, may last a lifetime. Relationships in the United States, in contrast, tend to be more short term.

3

Language Usage in the United States and Japan

In the previous chapter, we examined cultural similarities and differences between Japan and the United States. Our purpose in this chapter is to extend our analysis of how the two cultures are similar and different by focusing on selected aspects of communicating in English and Japanese. Language is important for several reasons. It is reciprocally related to culture; that is, our culture influences how we use language and our language usage influences how we view of our culture. Our language also influences how we look at the world and at the people in our culture.[1]

In a short book like this it is impossible to examine all aspects of the two languages.[2] Because this book is being written in English, we stress issues of communicating in Japanese since we assume those are less familiar to most readers. We divide the chapter into two broad sections. The first section focuses on differences between communicating in the two languages; the second emphasizes issues that arise when Japanese and North Americans speak each other's languages.

◆ Communicating in Japanese and English

In this section, we examine those areas of language usage that create the major problems in Japanese/North American intercultural communication. Many of the problems are due to different perceptions of the Japanese and English languages. Japanese speakers, for example, perceive Japanese to be (from most frequent to least frequent) delicate, polite, vague, gentle, abstract, poetic, warm, sensitive, and beautiful (Nisugi, 1974). Japanese speakers perceive English to be rhythmic, mechanical, modern, specific, objective, harsh, practical, systematic, and concise (Nisugi, 1974). English speakers, in contrast, perceive Japanese to be vague, polite, formal, abstract, and repetitious (Nisugi, 1974). English speakers perceive English to be warm, practical, concise, modern, forceful, sensitive, and objective (Nisugi, 1974).

To further explore differences in communication due to language, we examine how direct and indirect patterns of communication are a function of the language and how they are manifested in conversations. Next, we look at how the distinction between ingroups and outgroups is expressed in language. The third area we discuss is the functions of language: transmitting information versus persuading others. Following this, we look at how conversations are organized: topic management and turn taking. The fifth area we discuss involves the role of status in language usage. Finally, we look at the role of silence in conversations.

DIRECT VERSUS INDIRECT

As indicated in the previous chapter, the United States is an individualistic culture in which low-context messages tend to predominate, whereas Japan is a collectivistic culture in which high-context messages tend to predominate. When a person's goal is to assert him- or herself as a unique person (individualism), he or she must be direct so that others will know where he or she stands. If, on the other hand, a person's goal is to maintain harmony in the ingroup (collectivism), she or he cannot be direct because she or he might offend someone. To maintain harmony, collectivists need to be cautious and indirect.

Okabe (1983) contends that analytic thinking tends to predominate in the United States, whereas synthetic thinking tends to predominate in Japan. Analytic thinking involves looking at parts rather than focusing on the whole. Synthetic thinking, in contrast, involves trying to grasp things in their totality, in their "suchness." Constructing low-context messages requires analytic thinking, whereas constructing high-context messages involves synthetic thinking. Analytic thinking leads to the use of linear logic when talking or writing because it is necessary to specify how the parts are related to each other.[3] Synthetic thinking leads to a more "dotlike" logic. "The speaker organizes his or her ideas in a stepping-stone mode: The listener is supposed to supply what is left unsaid" (Okabe, 1983, p. 29).

These differences exist partly because English is a subject-centered language and Japanese is a predicate-centered language. Takabayashi (1986), for example, points out that "in English the subject is either an actor [or actress] or substance. Actor [or actress] controls the object to which his [or her] action is directed, and substance has quality" (p. 187). This requires the use of linear logic to connect the subject and the predicate. Takabayashi argues that the

> predicate-centeredness of Japanese means two things. First, . . . a subject is not always obligatory in a sentence. Second, in the topic-comment structure, topic is broader and more inclusive than the comment. This characteristic seems to be congenial with the idea that reality is complex and what we say about it amounts to be bits of comments, being a blurred and jerky picture of it. (p. 187)

Such a structure will not allow linear logic to be used.

Mizutani (1981) uses the example of a "higher-up" coming into a room that is cold and noticing that the window is open to illustrate how indirectness allows members of a group to maintain harmony. Although the higher-up might say something like *"'Samui-ja nai-ka, sono mado-o shimete-kure'* (Aren't you cold? Please close the window)" (p. 31), this language does not take into consideration the human relations among the group. The higher-up can avoid giving a direct order by saying something like "*samui-nee*" (It's cold in here) and hope that one of the people in the room understands the unspoken meaning and responds with "'*A, soo-ka, mado-ga akete-atta*' (Oh that's right. The window's open)" (p. 31). Mizutani argues that not all Japanese would respond indirectly in this situation, but that the majority of Japanese probably would unless there was a special relationship between themselves and the people in the room that would allow them to be direct.

Japanese often appears ambiguous to non-native speakers because the meaning of Japanese sentences must be determined within the situational context in which the sentences are uttered (or written). Mizutani (1981) provides several examples. If a guest enters a room (e.g., an office), the host may offer the guest a seat by just saying *doozo* (please). Clearly implied to another Japanese would be "have a seat." If the guest does not recognize that the word "please" is in a particular situational context, then he or she will be confused. To further illustrate this tendency, consider a situation where two people are out drinking and there is only beer on the table. If one person says to the other, "'*Nomimasen-ka*' (Won't you have [some]?)" (p. 48), it would be understood that the referent is beer. If the person says, "'*Biiru-o nomimasen-ka*' (Won't you have some beer?)" (p. 48), then the other person will understand that other drinks are available, but that the person making the offer has selected beer.

Interpreting sentences in context also is necessary to tell when Japanese are saying "no." Ueda (1974), for example, isolated 16 ways to say "no" in Japan. These include using a direct no, which is infrequent, using a vague no, giving a vague or ambiguous yes or no, using silence, using a counterquestion, giving a tangential response, exiting, lying or equivocating, criticizing, refusing to answer the question, giving a conditional no, saying "yes, but," delaying answering the question, stating regret, saying yes, and apologizing. The use of topic change is illustrated by the following exchange:

> **Foreign businessman:** Therefore, our products meet your requirements 100%. How soon do you think you can place an order?
>
> **Japanese businessman:** Did you see the *sumo* wrestling last night?
>
> **F.B.:** Well . . . Yes, I did. But back to our discussion, when would it be convenient . . . ?
>
> **J.B.:** What did you think of Jessie Takamiyama [a Hawaiian *sumo* wrestler]? Wasn't he terrific? (Imai, 1981, p. 8)

To understand that the Japanese is saying that he does not want to place an order, the foreign businessman must pay close attention to the context.

Another reason that the Japanese speak indirectly is the relatively low value that their culture places on words. Mizutani (1981) points out that

> the philosophy underlying the Japanese expectation toward words is definitely not "What is unsaid will not be understood" (*iwaneba waka-ranu*). Rather there seems to be distrust, with little hope placed on language—or at least the spoken language—as evidenced in such sentiments as "It should be understood without putting it into words" or "It's something that can't be understood even if put into words." (p. 78)

There are at least two related explanations for this low value placed on words and the use of indirect patterns of communication: the use of *awase*, or adjustive, logic (as opposed to *erabi*, or selective, logic that underlies direct forms of communication), and the distinction between *tatemae* (the standard to which one is bound in principle) and *honne* (one's true mind). Because *erabi* and *awase* were discussed in the previous chapter, we focus here on *tatemae* and *honne*.

Japanese draw a distinction between what is said in public (*tatemae*) and what one truly feels (*honne*). Yoshikawa (1978) observes that what is often verbally expressed and what is actually intended are two different things. What is verbally expressed is probably important enough to maintain friendship, and it is generally called "Tatemae" which means simply "in principle," but what is not verbalized counts most "Honne" which means "true mind." Although it is not expressed verbally, you are supposed to know it by "kan," "intuition." (p. 228)

Nishida (1977) argues that understanding what is not said when indirect forms of communication are used is left up to the listeners' *sasshi* (guessing what someone means) ability.

Before proceeding, it is important to recognize that indirectness occurs in the United States too. The reasons for indirectness in the two cultures, however, appear to be different. Condon (1984) quotes a professional interpreter in Japan as saying that

Americans can be just as indirect as the Japanese, but they are indirect about different things, and being indirect carries a different meaning. Americans are usually indirect when something very sensitive is being discussed or when they are nervous about how the other person might react. Whenever Americans are indirect, I suspect that *something* is going on!

Japanese indirectness is a part of our way of life. It is not because we are such kind and considerate people that we worry so about other's reactions. It is just that we know our own fates and fortunes are always bound up with others. I think you can value directness when you value individualism, or when you are with people you know and trust completely. (pp. 43-44)

North Americans are indirect at times and Japanese are direct. Japanese most frequently are direct in close friendships. We discuss this issue in more detail in the next chapter.

ROLE OF INGROUP AND
OUTGROUP IN CONVERSATION

There are many ways that insider and outsider status are marked in Japanese speech. Neustupny (1987), for example, points out that communication in the ingroup tends to be informal and involve a minimum use of honorifics. Communication with outgroup members, in contrast, tends to be more formal and involve the use of honorifics.

One marker between the ingroup and outgroup involves the phrases individuals use when talking. One example is the use of the common greeting *konnichi-wa*. Mizutani (1981) points out that typically people (both Japanese and non-Japanese studying Japanese) see *ohayoo* as a greeting used in the morning (or the first time you meet somebody during a day) and *konnichi-wa* as an afternoon greeting. He argues, however, that it is not this simple. Mizutani contends that *konnichi-wa* is not used with insiders, only with outsiders. To illustrate this, he tells a story of a father meeting his children a few years after the parents were divorced and the children had been living with their mother. The children greeted their father by saying *konnichi-wa,* clearly indicating to the father that he was now an outsider in their lives.[4]

Mizutani (1981) provides additional evidence regarding differences in how Japanese communicate with insiders and outsiders. He argues that greetings in Japan are not used to create new relationships with others. Rather, they are used to reaffirm existing social relationships. When strangers (outgroup members by definition) are encountered, they generally are not greeted. In the United States, greetings are used as a way to open the possibility of establishing a new relationship and recognizing the other person as an individual. When two strangers make eye contact, they usually greet each other even if they do not know each other. Inoue (1979) illustrates cultural differences in the use of greetings when he says:

> To take a typical phrase that a person uses at the time of introduction in American English, a person would say something like "How do you do? I'm pleased to meet you." or simply "Hello." In Japanese, a typical phrase begins with *hajime-mashite* which means something like "I'm meeting you for the first time." It is then followed by *doozo yoroshiku* which is a shortened version of the phrase that implies something like "Please do whatever you consider fit for

me." In other words, an introduction is an invitation, or an extension to the new acquaintance of the right to act for one's benefit.
It is an act of entrusting oneself to the other person. To an American,
this is clearly a separate step which might not take place until
long after initial greetings. (p. 280)

Given their views on introductions, Japanese, more than
North Americans, avoid strangers whose behavior may be
unpredictable.

Mizutani (1981) presents an interesting experiment to further
illustrate the differences in greetings when he went jogging one
morning. He greets all of the joggers (insiders) he encounters
while running around the Imperial Palace in Tokyo and he also
greets nonjoggers (outsiders). Virtually all of the joggers respond
to his greeting (95%), whereas only slightly more than half of
the nonjoggers (58%) respond to his greeting.

The emphasis on maintaining harmony and solidarity in the
ingroup in Japan can lead to negative behavior toward members
of outgroups (attacking outgroups is one way to increase ingroup cohesiveness). "By belittling a third person outside of the
group, one heightens insider solidarity and also reassures oneself of one's position as an insider" (Mizutani, 1981, p. 62).
Neustupny (1987) suggests that Japanese engage in criticism
with members of the ingroup who are not superiors, but that
they avoid criticism and conflict when communicating with
members of outgroups. Although this may be generally true,
conflict does occasionally occur with members of an outgroup,
and when it does, more individualistic styles can be used than
would be used with ingroup members. Cole (1990), for example,
found that Japanese use a dominating style to manage conflict
with members of an outgroup, whereas they use an integrating
style to manage conflicts with members of the ingroup.

Mizutani (1981) points out that the major insider-outsider
distinction that Japanese draw with respect to language is between Japanese and non-Japanese. This distinction, in combi-
nation with the preconception that non-Japanese can not speak
Japanese, influences the way that Japanese respond to non-

Japanese speaking English. This issue is discussed in detail below.

USING LANGUAGE TO TRANSMIT
INFORMATION AND TO PERSUADE

Mizutani (1981) argues that Japanese use language to transmit information to others, not persuade them. He believes that the average Japanese views persuading others as at least not high in value and possibly as something that should be avoided. There is an antipathy toward trying to get others to behave in a particular way. This is not to say that Japanese cannot persuade others, only that they prefer to avoid doing so if possible. One of the major reasons people communicate in the United States, in contrast, is to persuade or influence others. These differences are directly related to the *erabi* and *awase* views discussed earlier in the chapter.

The different orientations toward persuasion are reflected in the strategies people use when they have to engage in persuasion. To illustrate, Hirokawa and Miyahara (1986) examine the persuasive strategies used by North American and Japanese managers to persuade their subordinates in two situations.[5] The first situation involves how the manager tries to persuade consistently tardy employees to change their behavior. Japanese managers indicate that they appeal to the employees' sense of "duty" (e.g., "It is your duty as a responsible employee of this company to begin work on time"). The North American managers prefer to "threaten" the employees (e.g., "If you don't start reporting to work on time, I will have no choice but to dock your pay") or to give an ultimatum (e.g., "If you can't come to work on time, go find yourself another job").

The second situation in Hirokawa and Miyahara's study involves how the managers persuade employees to give their ideas and suggestions to managers. Japanese managers prefer to use "altruistic" strategies (e.g., "For the sake of the company, please share your ideas and suggestions with us") or appeal to "duty" (e.g., ""Remember that it is your duty as a good company

employee to suggest how we can improve the overall performance of the company"). The North American managers prefer
to make "direct requests" (e.g., "I want you to feel free to come
to me with any ideas you have for improving the company"), to
make "promises" (e.g., "Don't hesitate to offer ideas and suggestions because we always reward good suggestions"), or to "ingra-
tiate" themselves with the employees (e.g., "You are one of our
best people and I really value your judgment, so please feel free
to come to me with ideas you have").

Although Hirokawa and Miyahara's research on persuasive
strategy selection is not theoretically grounded, the results appear
compatible with cultural differences in individualism-collectivism. It would be expected, for example, that members of
collectivistic cultures would use persuasive strategies that are
altruistic or based on "duty" more than members of individualistic cultures.

TOPIC MANAGEMENT AND
TURN TAKING IN CONVERSATIONS

Yamada (1990) argues that the individual-group dimension
influences topic management and turn distribution in Japanese
and North American conversations.[6] She found that Japanese
"take short turns, distribute their turns relatively evenly, and
continue to distribute their turns evenly regardless of who
initiates a topic" (p. 291). North Americans, in contrast, "take
long monologic turns, distribute their turns unevenly, and the
participant who initiates a topic characteristically takes the
highest proportion of turns in that topic" (p. 291). Yamada
concludes that Japanese organize topics interdependently, whereas North Americans organize their topics independently. These
patterns can be linked directly to cultural differences in individualism and collectivism.

In her study of floor management, Hayashi (1990) finds that
Japanese use verbal and nonverbal complementary expressions
and repetition in floor support and maintenance negotiations.
North Americans, in contrast, use fewer syncronizing behav-

iors and repetition than Japanese. According to Hayashi, North Americans tend to use feedback devices (e.g., questions, comments) to indicate they are attentive, whereas Japanese tend to use backchanneling (e.g., *aizuchi*, brief utterances such as *soo* that make conversation flow smoothly) to accomplish this purpose. Hayashi also found that when North American "speakers orient attention, they focus on the specific topical content. Japanese speakers only value the emphatic interactional behavior and tend to consider the message exchange secondary" (p. 188).

Recent research also indicates that Japanese send backchannel signals to the person with whom they are communicating more than North American English speakers (e.g., White, 1989). Backchanneling also performs different functions in Japanese and English. Hayashi (1990), for example, argues that backchanneling is used to display understanding of content in English, whereas it is used mostly as an emphatic response and to indicate agreement in Japanese.[7] Backchanneling, however, can also be used to indicate understanding of content in Japanese.

The *aizuchi* used in Japanese include such words as *hai* (yes), *ee* (informal yes), *soo* (that's right), and *naruhodo nee* (indeed). Giving *aizuchi* does not mean that the listener agrees with the speaker, but rather that the listener is paying attention and urging the speaker to continue talking. If the listener does not provide *aizuchi* to the speaker in Japanese, holding a conversation becomes difficult. This can create problems when non-Japanese are learning Japanese. We discuss this issue later in this chapter.

Mizutani (1981) uses the metaphors of a volleyball game and a tennis match to explain Japanese conversations versus conversations in English. In English, people engaged in a conversation are like opponents in a tennis match: each hits the ball to the other person's side of the court and waits for him or her to return the ball. In Japanese conversations, in contrast, each person supports the other person by providing *aizuchi,* and there is give and take regarding the topic of conversation.

THE ROLE OF STATUS IN CONVERSATIONS

Okabe (1983) points out that English is a person-oriented language and Japanese is a status-oriented language. When context is not emphasized (e.g., as in English), messages must be adapted to the specific person with whom people are communicating. When context is important (e.g., as in Japanese), messages must take the context into consideration. In Japan a large part of the context is the relationship between the two persons.

The honorific forms (*keigo*) of the language that Japanese use in conversations depend on whether the person to whom one is speaking is above or below the speaker in social status. If the listener is above the speaker in social status or age and the speaker is talking about the listener's actions, respect forms of *keigo* (*sonkeigo*) must be used. In this situation, if the speaker is referring to his or her own actions, humble forms of *keigo* (*kenjoogo*) must be used. Mizutani (1981) points out that Japanese are very strict about correct usage of *sonkeigo* and *kenjoogo* and that failure to use them correctly will lead to criticism.

Suzuki (1978) illustrates how status differences influence the terms of address individuals use in the United States and Japan. He points out that

> when American graduate students earn their doctorates, they soon start calling their former professors by their first names. The reason is that in the United States the concept of colleagueship is an egalitarian one and supersedes differences in seniority, scholarship, or age. In contrast, I still cannot call an old professor by any term other than *Sensei,* "Teacher." This is more than twenty years after graduation. The fact that specific Japanese interpersonal pairs are fixed in terms of the role of each member and are virtually immune to changes of situation and passage of time. (pp. 162-163)

Adjusting one's communication to the status of those present in the situation is one of the major dimensions to emerge in Gudykunst, Gao, Nishida, Nadamitsu, and Sakai's (1992) study of self-monitoring in Japan and the United States. Japanese score higher on this dimension than North Americans.

SILENCE IN CONVERSATIONS

Recent research suggests that there are specific cultural differences regarding "beliefs about talk." Beliefs about talk refer to our evaluations of the functions of talk and silence (Wiemann, Chen, & Giles, 1986). Triandis (cited in Giles, Coupland, & Wiemann, 1992) argues that cultural differences in beliefs about talk are due to individualism-collectivism:

> Individualists have a choice among many groups . . . to which they do belong, and usually belong to these groups because they volunteer. Collectivists . . . are born into a few groups and are more or less stuck with them. So, the collectivists do not have to go out of their way and exert themselves to be accepted, while individualists have to work hard to be accepted. Hence, the individualists often speak more, try to control the situation verbally, and do not value silence. (p. 11)

Triandis' argument about beliefs about talk appears to generalize to understanding Japanese communication.

Mizutani (1981) contends that although Japanese have become more talkative in recent years, not talking too much is still viewed as a "mark of adulthood." He goes on to point out that there is tremendous situational variability when Japanese are talkative. One person may be quiet at work and talkative at home, whereas another may be talkative at work and not talk much in the family. Tsujimura (1987) believes that *ishin-denshin* (taciturnity) is one of the major characteristics of Japanese communication. This involves not talking a lot. When carried to an extreme, *ishin-denshin* involves communication without talking, mental telepathy. This often is equated with *haragei* (belly to belly) communication (see Okabe, 1983).

Neustupny (1987) isolates several reasons why Japanese talk less than North Americans. First, when there is a senior person present in a situation, it is up to the superior to initiate speech. Unless the superior begins a conversation, silence is appropriate. Second, if there are members of an outgroup present, talk is difficult. Third, the sex of the people present influences the amount of talk. Talk takes places more when only members of the same sex are present than in opposite-sex groups (see our discussion of masculinity-femininity in Chapter 2). Fourth, some situations do not demand talk. When having lunch in a company lunch room, for example, Japanese may not speak, even though they speak before or after eating. Finally, there are situations where people may just have little to say. Waiting at a bus stop with an acquaintance or at a party are examples of these situations in Japan.

Lebra (1987) isolates four meanings of what can be conveyed by silence in Japan: truthfulness, social discretion, embarrassment, and defiance.[8] With respect to truthfulness, it is important to recognize that Japanese draw a distinction between inner and outer aspects of life (e.g., *tatemae/honne, uchi/soto*). Lebra argues that Japanese view truth as occurring only in the inner realms, which are symbolically located in the belly or heart. Activities regarding the outer self (e.g., *tatemae*) do not involve an individual's true feelings and therefore frequently involve distortion, deception, or "moral falsity." True feelings (*honne*) are on the inside of a person. A person who speaks little is trusted more than a person who speaks a lot. Truthfulness emerges from silences, not words in Japan.

Silence also allows Japanese to be socially discreet. "Social discretion refers to silence considered necessary or desirable in order to gain social acceptance or to avoid social penalty" (Lebra, 1987, p. 347). At times talking may be dangerous and require that the person tell the truth. In these instances silence allows the person to avoid social disapproval. In these situations, "silence is sometimes associated even by Japanese with inscrutability, concealment, sneakiness, disguise, and dangerousness, paradoxically, in the same fashion as speech is in the first dimension" (p. 348).

Silence also saves Japanese from being embarrassed. Verbally expressing emotions to each other, for example, may cause a married couple to become embarrassed. They therefore avoid being embarrassed by being silent. Silence saves people from embarrassment in intimate situations. The final way silence is used is to be defiant or to express estrangement. A person may indicate disagreement or anger with someone else by being silent.

Lebra (1987) suggests that the opposite meanings in the use of silence in Japan can create confusion to cultural outsiders. The confusion, however, is not limited to outsiders. She points out that

> when a woman says she was silent throughout the period of her husband's extramarital indulgence, she can mean her feminine modesty, compliance, patience, resentment, unforgivingness, or defiance, and may mean all. A man's refusal to express tender feelings toward his wife may be explained not only as embarrassment, but as an expression of male dignity, or as his true, sincere love which is beyond words. (p. 350)

Differentiating among the various explanations depends on the nonverbal cues in the particular situation.

◆ Second Language Competence

In the previous section we examined a few of the differences between communicating in Japanese and English. Our purpose in this section is to look at issues that arise when Japanese speak English and North Americans speak Japanese. We begin by looking at Japanese speaking English.

JAPANESE SPEAKING ENGLISH

English is a compulsory subject for junior and senior high school students in Japan. The focus of language instruction, however, is on preparing students for the college entrance examinations. Teachers, therefore, emphasize reading, grammar, and vocabulary, not spoken English. "A good [English] teacher is a teacher who is able to mold his [or her] students into successful candidates for prestigious universities" (Yoshima & Sasatami, 1980, p. 11). The main motivation for students' learning English is instrumental: it will help them accomplish their goals.

Given the way it is taught in schools, English is not *spoken* widely in Japan. It is spoken in international hotels and tourist locations, but not by the population at large. This should not be surprising because there is little opportunity for the average Japanese to speak English. Many companies, however, include sections on English in employment exams and offer English conversation classes to employees. Some companies also require employees to attain a certain competence in English to be promoted to certain positions in the organization. Thus the motivation of employees to learn English, like the motivation of students, is instrumental.

Neustupny (1987) argues that the major reason that Japanese do not speak English is the tremendous dissimilarities between English and Japanese. Hildebrandt and Giles (1980) suggest that the need for a positive cultural identity also plays an important role in why Japanese do not learn to speak English. They point out that "the prevailing attitudes in Japan would tend to discourage confidence and encourage the feeling of 'shyness' professed by many Japanese in foreign language interactions. This lack of confidence would further enhance the need for differentiation from the outgroup [native English speakers] to increase a positive social identity" (p. 78). Stated differently, if Japanese do not feel confident speaking English, then they need to differentiate themselves from English speakers (e.g., by not speaking English) in order to have a positive cultural identity.

Ability to speak English can have an influence on a Japanese's cultural identity.[9] To illustrate, Japanese who speak English "like a native" often are perceived negatively by other Japanese (Honne, 1980). In other words, speaking English well can subtract from Japanese's cultural identity. This, however, is not always the case. San Antonio (1987) studied the use of Japanese and English in a U.S. corporation in Japan. She found that those who spoke English well were viewed positively by the North American workers. These Japanese also were viewed positively by the other Japanese working for the company who did not speak English well. The Japanese who spoke English well were able to protect the Japanese employees who did not speak

English well from embarrassment by speaking up at meetings and answering North Americans' questions. How Japanese who speak English well are perceived by other Japanese is a function of the other person's attitude toward English and the specific situational context in which Japanese are speaking English.

Although English is not spoken widely in Japan, when Japanese and North Americans communicate, conversations most frequently take place in English. One reason for this is that few North Americans speak sufficient Japanese to hold a conversation. Another reason is that English often is thought of as the "international language." Tsuda (1986) argues that there are problems with treating English as the international language. He points out that "the use of English causes cultural and ideological bias in communication" (p. 49). A language is *not* just a medium of communication, "it represents the soul, ideology, and the way of life of the English-speaking people" (p. 49).

One illustration of the role of language in the way people think about the world is how bilinguals answer questions asked in Japanese and English differently. Ervin-Tripp (1964, p. 96), for example, asked the same questions on different days in Japanese and English to Japanese women who were bilingual. One woman's responses were as follows:

1. WHEN MY WISHES CONFLICT WITH MY FAMILY . . .
   (Japanese) it is a time of great unhappiness.
   (English) I do what I want.
2. I WILL PROBABLY BECOME . . .
   (Japanese) a housewife.
   (English) a teacher.
3. REAL FRIENDS SHOULD . . .
   (Japanese) help each other.
   (English) be very frank.

These responses clearly indicate that different approaches to the world emerge when Japanese bilinguals think in Japanese and English. It should be noted, however, that Japanese world-views do not disappear when speaking in English. Beebe and

Takahashi (1989), for example, argue that many Japanese perform face-threatening acts in a Japanese fashion in English.

NORTH AMERICANS SPEAKING JAPANESE

The number of people studying Japanese has increased in
recent years. There are, however, few North Americans who
speak Japanese fluently. Even if North Americans speak Japanese
well or fluently, it does not ensure effective communication
with Japanese.

Mizutani (1981) points out that many non-Japanese studying
Japanese in Japan become frustrated when they speak Japanese
in everyday situations and the Japanese with whom they are
speaking do not recognize that they are speaking Japanese. To
illustrate, a non-Japanese may ask people at the train station, in
perfect Japanese, where the train goes, and the Japanese will
respond by waving their hands in front of their faces to indicate
that they do not understand. The non-Japanese tends to assume
that something is wrong with his or her Japanese, but Mizutani
contends that it often is a function of the Japanese preconception about non-Japanese's use of Japanese. "Many Japanese have
the preconception that anything coming out of a white foreigner's mouth is English or some other foreign language they cannot
understand. Even if those foreigners should be speaking Japanese, they will deny this fact because they think a foreigner
cannot possibly be speaking Japanese" (Mizutani, 1981, p. 65).
This is a reflection of the general tendency for people to confirm
their expectations when they communicate with people from
other groups (see Stephan, 1985). It should be noted, however,
that attitudes toward non-Japanese who are fluent in Japanese
may be changing, especially in the large metropolitan areas.
This issue will be discussed in more detail in Chapter 5.

Several writers (e.g., Jorden, 1977; Miller, 1977) argue that
Japanese tend to linguistically diverge from non-Japanese who
speak Japanese. One writer (Miller, 1977) proposes the "law
of inverse returns" with respect to non-Japanese learning
Japanese:

> This law holds that the better you get at the language, the less credit you are given for your accomplishments; the more fluently you speak it, the less hard won skills will do for you in making friends and favorably impressing people; but by the same token the less you can do with the language, the more you will be praised and encouraged by Japanese society in general and your friends in particular. (p. 78)

Many critics disagree with Miller's position (e.g., Allen, 1983). These critics suggest that the attitude Miller describes toward non-Japanese use of Japanese may have been true in earlier times (e.g., the late 1950s and early 1960s), but has disappeared in current Japanese society. One survey (Saint Jacques, 1983) supports this view. The survey revealed that 97% of the non-Japanese surveyed thought Japanese had a favorable impression of non-Japanese speaking Japanese. Unfortunately, this survey did not control for the fluency level of the individuals surveyed.

Like North American responses to Japanese speaking English, Japanese respond to North Americans speaking Japanese with a version of "foreigner talk":

> Foreigners who do not possess a semi-native competence must accept that the Japanese used toward them will be more or less a weaker or stronger variety of Foreigner Talk. For instance, few honorifics will be used, pronouns (*watashi* "I," *anata* "you") may appear with increased frequency, English words may replace Japanese words, and conversational topics may be simplified. The style of speech will be careful and slow and Standard forms may appear instead of Common Japanese. (Neustupny, 1987, p. 163)

It is important to keep in mind that the use of foreigner talk is not limited to Japanese speaking Japanese with non-Japanese. North Americans use foreigner talk with Japanese speaking English as well. Extreme foreigner talk in either situation can create a large communicative distance between the communicators.

Another area where problems occur when non-Japanese are speaking Japanese is in the use of *aizuchi*. As we indicated, *aizuchi* is used frequently in Japanese conversations as a way for the listener to let the speaker know that he or she is listening.

When the non-native speaker is not aware of the rules for using *aizuchi*, it can create problems. Mizutani (1981, pp. 83-84) provides the following example to illustrate this point:

> *Japanese: Moshi moshi.* (Hello.)
> *Foreigner: Moshi moshi.* (Hello.)
> *Japanese: Ee, kochira, anoo, Yamamoto-desu-ga.* (Uuh, this is err, Yamamoto.)
> *Foreigner:* . . .
> *Japanese: Moshi moshi.* (Are you there?)
> *Foreigner: Moshi moshi.* (Hello.)
> *Japanese: Kochira, Yamamoto-desu-ga. Johnsonsan-wa* . . . (This is Yamamoto. Is Mr./Ms. Johnson . . .)
> *Foreigner:* . . .
> *Japanese: Moshi moshi.* (Are you there?)

The caller identifies himself in the third line and expects that the listener would provide *aizuchi* to indicate that he or she is paying attention. When no *aizuchi* is provided the caller assumes that the listener was not following the conversation. The caller, therefore, uses *moshi moshi* to determine if the listener is still there. This pattern is repeated later in the conversation when no *aizuchi* is provided. LoCastro (1987) observes that when non-Japanese are able to use *aizuchi* it decreases misunderstandings.

When North Americans are in Japan, it is important for them to recognize that they cannot always follow the old advice "When in Rome, act as a Roman." If non-Japanese act as Japanese (including language usage) in Japan, they are viewed as strange. A Japanese journalist points out that

> foreigners in Japan should avoid the extremes of adjustment—not trying at all or trying too much. If they make no effort to adjust to Japanese ways [including language usage], they are simply tolerated. If they are like Japanese in every way except for appearance, they are regarded as strange—unless their background is known, such as *gaijin* who grew up in Japan. Foreigners working

in Japan are at their best when they "behave with an accent." (quoted in Condon, 1984, p. 19)

Non-Japanese in Japan, therefore, need to learn to speak some Japanese and adapt to some Japanese patterns of behavior in order to communicate successfully in Japan. We discuss these issues in more detail in Chapter 6.

Notes

1. We are taking a position consistent with the "weak" version of the Sapir-Whorf hypothesis (Whorf, 1956). Language influences, but does not determine, how we view the world.

2. For a more detailed analysis see Akasu and Asano (1993).

3. See Hinds (1983) for an analysis of rhetoric in writing in Japanese and English.

4. Mizutani also points out that there is a similar pattern in the use of *oyasumi-nasai* (good night) and *konban-wa* (good evening). While *oyasumi-nasai* can be used with both members of the ingroup and the outgroup, *konban-wa* is only used with members of outgroups.

5. There are other studies of persuasive strategy selection in Japan and the United States. There are, however, methodological problems with these studies that make their findings difficult to interpret. Neulip and Hazelton (1985), for example, studied Japanese and North Americans, but the research instrument administered in Japan was in English.

6. For an extensive discussion of topic management in business meetings, see Yamada (in press).

7. See Hayashi (1988) for a discussion of differences in use of simultaneous talk in English and Japanese.

8. See Morsbach (1988b) for an alternative discussion of silence.

9. The term *kokusaijin* ("international people") often is used to refer to Japanese who speak English (or other foreign languages) and have frequent contact with foreigners.

4

Communication Patterns in the United States and Japan

In the previous two chapters, we examined how the cultures of the United States and Japan are similar and different and discussed how language influences communication in the two cultures. In this chapter, we extend our analysis by comparing communication patterns in the two cultures. We begin by looking at similarities and differences in communication in interpersonal and intergroup relationships. Following this, we examine more specific aspects of communication such as communicator styles and attitudes toward verbal messages. We conclude this chapter by summarizing the limited research on what happens when Japanese and North Americans communicate.

◆ Communication in Interpersonal and Intergroup Relationships

In this section, we examine general patterns of communication in relationships. We begin with initial interactions. Next, we look at communication in developing relationships. We conclude by discussing how communication in ingroups and outgroups is different.

INITIAL INTERACTIONS

North Americans communicate more frequently with strangers than Japanese do (Barnlund, 1989). In this section, we examine three aspects of communication in initial interactions: uncertainty reduction, self-disclosure, and nonverbal communication.

Uncertainty Reduction

Gudykunst and Nishida (1986a) argue that reducing uncertainty is a major concern in Japanese interpersonal relationships.
This position is based on the work of Japanese researchers (e.g.,
Nakane, 1974) and on Hofstede's (1980) dimensions of cultural
variability (i.e., Japan has a high score on the uncertainty avoidance dimension). There are, however, different factors that are
important in reducing uncertainty in Japan and the United States.
One area where there are differences is the relative emphasis
placed on verbal and nonverbal aspects of communication in
reducing uncertainty. Japanese communication focuses more
on nonverbal aspects of communication than communication
in the United States does (Kunihiro, 1976; Tsujimura, 1987),
whereas North American communication focuses more on the
verbal message than Japanese communication does (Gudykunst
& Nishida, 1986a).[1] Tsujimura (1987), for example, argues that
much of Japanese communication is based on (1) *ishin-denshin*
("traditional mental telepathy"), (2) taciturnity, (3) *kuuki* (mood
or atmosphere), and (4) respect for reverberation (indirect
communication).[2] Ito (1989b) argues that Japanese need to be
sensitive to others' true feelings because Japanese attitudes are
"double structured" (i.e., Japanese draw a distinction between
tatemae, diplomatic attitude or the attitude expressed to others, and *honne*, true attitude). *Tatemae* is expressed verbally;
honne must be determined indirectly.

Because of the emphasis on indirect verbal communication
and nonverbal communication, members of collectivistic cultures
like Japan need to know whether others understand them when
they do not verbally express their feelings in order to reduce

uncertainty. It also is necessary for members of collectivistic cultures to know whether others will make allowances for them when they communicate and for them to have confidence in predicting others' behavior. The concept of *sasshi* illustrates this claim. Nishida (1977) defines *sasshi* as meaning conjecture, surmise, or guessing what someone means. In its verb form (*sassuru*), its meaning is expanded to include imagining, supposing, empathizing with, and making allowances for others. Although nonverbal sensitivity to indirect forms of communication is necessary to reduce uncertainty in Japan, it is information about others' attitudes, beliefs, values, and so forth that is necessary to reduce uncertainty for direct communication used in the United States.

The second area where there are differences in how Japanese and North Americans reduce uncertainty is in the relative emphasis placed on person-based and group-based information (Gudykunst & Nishida, 1986a). North Americans focus on information specific to the individuals with whom they are communicating in order to reduce their uncertainty about using direct forms of communication. North Americans seek information about others' attitudes, values, beliefs, and so forth in order to be able to predict their behavior. Japanese, in contrast, focus on group-based information to reduce their uncertainty. Japanese need to know others' group memberships (e.g., for whom they work), age, status, and so forth in order to predict their behavior.

Both person-based and group-based information are used in the United States and Japan. Japanese use information on individuals' attitudes, beliefs, and feelings, but this information appears to be secondary to the nonverbal and group-based information necessary to reduce uncertainty in indirect forms of communication. Similarly, North Americans use information on whether others understand their feelings or will make allowances for them, but this information is secondary to the others' attitudes, values, and beliefs. Frequency of communication increases the possibility of uncertainty reduction in the United States more than in Japan. But in Japan, more than in the United

States, overlap in social networks and interacting with members of the other person's social network, in contrast, help individuals know whether others will make allowances for them.

With respect to uncertainty reduction in initial interactions, Japanese are able to reduce uncertainty about strangers' behavior when provided background information (e.g., school attended) more than North Americans (Gudykunst & Nishida, 1984; Nishida & Gudykunst, 1986a). Background information provides a solid foundation on which to make predictions about others' behavior in collectivistic cultures like Japan, but not in individualistic cultures like the United States. Nakane (1974) tells a story that illustrates this point. She taught at Tokyo University, but was visiting another university to give a lecture. She was anxious about the situation because she did not know anyone at the university where she was lecturing. When she walked into the lecture hall another professor was waiting to greet her. Before he said anything else to her, the professor said, "I'm from Tokyo," meaning he had attended Tokyo University. Nakane reports that this one piece of information (knowing that they shared a major ingroup membership) allowed her to reduce her uncertainty about the other professor and feel comfortable interacting with him. The same information in the United States would not produce the same degree of reduction in uncertainty. In fact, it might be argued that there is no one single piece of information about another person that will reduce uncertainty to the same degree in the United States.

Self-Disclosure

One of the areas where there are differences between Japanese and North Americans involves the amount of self-disclosure that takes place. As indicated earlier, North Americans need person-based information about others in order to reduce their uncertainty. This information can be gathered in three major ways: it can be volunteered by the other person, questions can be asked of the other person (North Americans ask more questions

.

of strangers than Japanese; Gudykunst & Nishida, 1984), or the person reducing uncertainty can disclose information about him- or herself. Self-disclosure provides information about the other person because of the reciprocity norm (Gouldner, 1960). The reciprocity norm suggests that if one person tells another information about him- or herself, the other person will reciprocate and tell the same information about her- or himself.

Overall, North Americans self-disclose more than Japanese (Barnlund, 1975, 1989). This pattern is consistent across topics of conversation and target persons (Barnlund, 1975, 1989). Although there are differences in the amount of self-disclosure, there are similarities in what is disclosed. Tastes and opinions are viewed as the most appropriate topics for conversation in Japan and the United States, whereas physical attributes and personal traits are viewed as the least appropriate (Barnlund, 1975, 1989). The hierarchy of preferred target persons is the same in the two cultures: same-sex friend, opposite-sex friend, mother, father, stranger, and untrusted acquaintance.

Nishida (1991) contends that there are both similarities and differences between North American and Japanese students in the topics of self-disclosure in the first five minutes of initial interactions.[3] In the first five minutes, North American students in his study would discuss the weather, names, immediate surroundings, time, academic majors, current courses, destinations, universities, mutual friends, surrounding activities, and home towns. The corresponding topics for Japanese students are the weather, names, universities, ages, home towns, academic majors, destinations, addresses, time, living arrangements, immediate surroundings, mutual friends, and commuting. Nine of the topics (out of 11 total for North Americans and 13 total for Japanese) are common in the two samples. This study, therefore, is consistent with Barnlund's (1975, 1989) research.

Miyanaga (1991) provides an explanation for the differences in self-disclosure based on the Japanese conception of *tatemae* and *honne*. She argues that *honne* is what a person really wants to do, and *tatemae* is his [or her] submission to moral obligation. Interaction rituals begin with mutual expressions that are culturally prescribed when two parties meet; they develop from occasional (i.e., formal) to frequent (i.e., intimate) exposure of honest feelings. The particularities of the moral basis of interaction rituals is socially established and agreed upon. Honest feelings, however, are, by definition, personal. Premature expression of honest expectations can incite a strongly negative response from the other person in the relationship. (p. 89)

In collectivistic cultures like Japan, individuals do not expose their true feelings until they know another person well. In individualistic cultures, individuals are expected to express themselves to others even if they do not know them well.

Nonverbal Aspects of Communication

It is not only verbal aspects of communication that differ in initial interactions. Japanese display more nonverbal behavior to strangers than do North Americans (Gudykunst & Nishida, 1984). This is consistent with predictions based on Hofstede's (1980) uncertainty avoidance dimension; members of high uncertainty avoidance cultures (e.g., Japan) display emotions more than members of low uncertainty avoidance cultures (e.g., the United States). If the high uncertainty avoidance culture is also collectivistic, however, it would be expected that the emotions displayed would be limited to "positive" emotions because "negative" emotions are not conducive to maintaining group harmony. Friesen's (1972) research illustrates this point. He finds that students in Japan and the United States display similar affect in response to a stressful film when viewing it alone, but that when in the company of a peer, those from the United States show more negative affect than those from Japan. Similarly, Argyle, Henderson, Bond, Iizuka, and Contarelo (1986) find that the English and Italians (both individualistic cultures) display more anger and distress than Japanese.

When speaking their native language, Japanese sit further apart when communicating with strangers than North Americans

(Sussman & Rosenfeld, 1982). When speaking English, however, the distance that Japanese sit from each other approximates that used in the United States. Japanese also prefer greater interaction distances with their friends, fathers, and professors than do Caucasians in the United States (Engebretson & Fullmer, 1970).[4]

The areas where North Americans and Japanese touch each other tend to be relatively similar. The hand, forehead, shoulder, back of the neck or head, and forearm are the most frequent areas touched, whereas the pelvis area, rear of the thigh, and back of the lower leg are the least touched (Barnlund, 1975). The people touched also are relatively similar. Japanese touch opposite-sex friends the most, followed by mothers and same-sex friends, and fathers the least. There is not much overall difference in how much opposite-sex friends, mothers, and same-sex friends are touched. In the United States opposite-sex friends are touched the most, followed by mothers, same-sex friends, and fathers. Fathers and same-sex friends are touched about the same amount, and there is a large difference between how much same-sex and opposite-sex friends are touched. It should be noted, however, that opposite-sex friends are touched more in the United States than in Japan. Overall, North Americans touch each other about twice as much as Japanese (Barnlund, 1975).

Another area where nonverbal behavior differs in Japan and the United States is with respect to time. Hall and Hall (1987) differentiate between monochronic and polychronic time. In monochronic systems "time is experienced and used in a linear way" (p. 16). In cultures where monochronic time predominates like the United States, the emphasis is on doing one thing at a time, meeting deadlines, having schedules and plans, and being prompt. The emphasis in cultures where polychronic time predominates is on doing many things at the same time, focusing on people rather than task completion, and *not* emphasizing schedules, deadlines, and plans. Hall and Hall point out that Japanese tend to use monochronic time when dealing with foreigners, but use polychronic time in their interpersonal relations.

DEVELOPING RELATIONSHIPS

The patterns of how relationships develop are relatively similar in Japan and the United States. There are, however, variations in communication within stages of relationship development. In this section, we examine three aspects of developing relationships: stages of relationship development, perceptions of communication within relationships, and privacy regulation.

Stages of Relationship Development

Social penetration theory (Altman & Taylor, 1973) posits four stages of relationship development: orientation, exploratory affective exchange, affective exchange, and stable exchange. The orientation stage is characterized by responses that are stereotypical and reflect superficial aspects of the personalities of the individuals involved in a relationship. Exploratory affective exchange involves interaction at the periphery of the personality of the partners. This stage includes relationships that are friendly and relaxed, but features limited or temporary commitments. The third stage, full affective exchange, involves "loose" and "free-wheeling" interaction and an increase of self-disclosure in central areas of the partners' personalities. Stable exchange, the final stage, emerges when partners have fully described themselves to each other and involves few instances of miscommunication.

Though the stages of relationship development were isolated in the United States, they appear to be applicable to interpersonal relationships in Japan. To illustrate, Japanese and North Americans agree on the ratings of the intimacy for five terms used to describe interpersonal relationships (from least to most intimate): stranger, acquaintance, friend, close friend, and best friend (Gudykunst & Nishida, 1986b). These data support the generalizability of the stages of social penetration theory (Altman & Taylor, 1973) across cultures.

Miyanaga (1991) provides a description of the stages of Japanese relationships that is similar to those posited in social penetration theory. She also points out, however, that there are differences in the communication that occurs within each stage. Miyanaga argues that Japanese strive for "perfect mutual understanding" in personal relationships and that this is possible because of the "interaction rituals" that take place in all stages of a personal relationship. A large part of the interaction rituals in Japanese personal relationships involves nonverbal cues. Miyanaga contends that communicators'

> body movements, tone of voice, degree of avoidance of eye contact, laughter, smiles, serious expressions, and even the degree of body tension are, to a certain extent, carefully controlled to constitute cues.
>
> At the same time, a person tries as much as possible to catch the cues given by others. If a person keeps missing the given cues, he [or she] will be judged as "blunt" or "dull" (because he [or she] is unreceptive), "impolite" (when it is judged that he [or she] is deliberately choosing to miss cues), or *gaijin mitai* (like a foreigner). High receptivity is admired. The Japanese word generally used to indicate such receptivity is *sasshi*, which literally means "to guess." It implies that one guesses the real intention of others in spite of their surface disguise. . . .
>
> Although a high *sasshi* ability in the recipient of cues is much appreciated, an expectation of *sasshi* effort from the other is discouraged. The word for this is *amae*. Although *amae* has been co-opted as a psychological concept by Takeo Doi (1973), in the interaction ritual it is simply used to indicate the restriction of excessive dependency on the *sasshi* of the other person. . . . *Amae*, when used in a conversation, signifies a passive aggression in which one depends on the manners of others. (pp. 85-86)

Miyanaga goes on to argue that in an "ideal" relationship where *sasshi* and *amae* are operating, Japanese communicate spontaneously. Each partner in a relationship understands when the other will follow behavior norms and when the other will abandon the behavioral norms. As relationships become more intimate, the interaction rituals used by the partners become more idiosyncratic. This idea is similar to Miller and Steinberg's (1975) argument that the rule structures guiding relationships become more idiosyncratic as relationships become more intimate.

Perceptions of Communication Within Relationships

Perceptions of communication in relationships in the United States and Japan vary along three dimensions: personalization, synchronization, and difficulty (Knapp, Ellis, & Williams, 1980; Gudykunst & Nishida, 1986b). Personalized communication involves the intimacy of communication (e.g., "We tell each other personal things about ourselves—things we don't tell most people"). Synchronized communication relates to the coordination of communication between partners (e.g., "Due to mutual cooperation, our conversations are generally effortless and smooth flowing"). Difficulty of communication encompasses barriers to communication (e.g., "It is difficult for us to know when the other person is being serious or sarcastic"). Communication becomes more personalized and synchronized and less difficulty is experienced as relationships become more intimate in both cultures.

Though patterns of social penetration are similar, there are differences in how intimate Japanese and North Americans perceive different relationships to be. Japanese, for example, rate relationship terms associated with two of their ingroups (university classmates and co-workers) as more intimate than North Americans do. Japanese also perceive family relationship terms as less intimate than North Americans do. In collectivistic cultures where the family is not ranked as the most important ingroup, family relationships should not be perceived as highly intimate; Nakane (1970, 1974) argues that Japanese rate the company ingroup first. The ratings of opposite-sex relationship terms are consistent with Hofstede's (1980) masculinity dimension. Specifically, opposite-sex terms are rated as less intimate by Japanese than by North Americans. Since highly masculine cultures like Japan have strong sex-role differentiation, there is little informal contact between males and females (see White, 1993, for a recent discussion). Consistent with this line of thinking, Japanese select a same-sex friend as their closest relationship, whereas North Americans select their romantic partners (Gudykunst & Nishida, 1993).

As interpersonal relationships become more intimate, there should be few cultural differences in the nature of communication that takes place.[5] This assumption is supported, in part, by descriptions of communication in close friendships in Japan. Vogel (1963), for example, argues that in true friendships, "people are relaxed and do not worry about formalities. They can talk and joke about their innermost concerns. . . . With close friends, one can argue, criticize, and be stubborn without endangering the relationships. . . . These relationships are remarkably intimate" (p. 136). Atsumi (1980) also points out that the number of friendship relationships is small in Japan (less than half a dozen), that they usually are with members of the same sex, and that they also generally are with former classmates. Some friendship relationships are *shinyuu* (intimate friendships). In these relationships, Japanese feel "completely open and relaxed" (p. 70). White (1993) found similar patterns of communication in close friendships in Japan and the United States. One of her informants, for example, says that "being with my [best friend] I can have deep discussions without . . . putting on airs and worrying about how the other will feel" (p. 145). It should be noted, however, that close friendships in Japan tend to be relationships established early in life and are often lifelong relationships.

Friendships in Japan and the United States share many common characteristics. The four most frequently mentioned characteristics in Japan are togetherness, trust, warmth, and understanding. The corresponding characteristics in the United States are understanding, respect/sincerity, trust, and helping (Takahara, 1974). There appear to be differences, however, in the characteristics Japanese and North Americans look for in mates. North Americans look for intelligence, physical attraction, sex appeal, affection, trust, and psychological support in mates. Japanese, in comparison, look for intelligence, health, honesty, affection, common values, the ease with which they can talk to the partner, and how good the partner is with handling money (Cushman & Nishida, 1983).[6]

There are a few minor differences in communication in close friendships in Japan and the United States. North Americans, for example, engage in more social penetration with close friends regarding their own marriage and family, love and dating, and emotions and feelings than Japanese (Gudykunst & Nishida, 1983). These differences appear to be due to differences in maculinity-femininity. Members of highly masculine cultures (e.g., Japan) discuss topics dealing with opposite-sex relationships less than people in cultures lower on the masculinity index (e.g., the United States). The sex of the person with whom an individual is communicating (i.e., a male or a female) also influences how relationships develop. Unreported data from Gudykunst, Yang, and Nishida's (1985) study support the argument outlined here.

Privacy

Privacy regulation is a process through which individuals make themselves accessible or inaccessible to others (Altman, 1977). People in all cultures regulate privacy, but the specific mechanisms people use vary across cultures (Altman, 1977).

Japanese are more likely to use lack of attentiveness as a privacy control mechanism than North Americans. Japanese also are more likely to indirectly tell others they want privacy than are North Americans (Baker & Gudykunst, 1990). Japanese also prefer "passive-withdrawal" strategies when confronted with a threat to the self. North Americans, in contrast, prefer "active-aggressive" strategies (Barnlund, 1975). Further, Japanese avoid direct confrontation and use indirect strategies when their privacy is threatened by others (Naotsuka & Sakamoto, 1981).

INGROUP AND OUTGROUP RELATIONSHIPS

Both Japanese and North Americans perceive intergroup encounters as more abrasive and less agreeable than interpersonal encounters (Gudykunst, Nishida, & Morisaki, 1992). Members of collectivistic cultures, nevertheless, draw a sharper distinction between ingroup and outgroup communication than members of individualistic cultures (Triandis, 1988). Consistent with this view, Japanese report greater differences in personalization and synchronization and greater difficulty of communication between ingroup (classmate) and outgroup (stranger) relationships than North Americans do (Gudykunst & Nishida, 1986b; Gudykunst, Yoon, & Nishida, 1987). Similarly, Japanese have less uncertainty regarding the behavior of classmates (members of an ingroup in Japan) than the behavior of strangers (potential members of an outgroup in Japan). There are no differences in uncertainty regarding classmates and strangers in the United States (Gudykunst & Nishida, 1986a; Gudykunst, Nishida, & Schmidt, 1989; Gudykunst, Gao, Schmidt, Nishida, Bond, Leung, Wang, & Barraclough, 1992).

There is further support for the argument outlined here in two studies replicating Asch's (1956) classic studies of conformity in Japan. Frager (1970) finds that levels of conformity are low in Japan (in fact, the conformity was lower than in Asch's study in the United States) when the confederates in the study are strangers (i.e., not members of an ingroup). More recently, Williams and Sogon (1984) observe that when confederates are members of the respondents' ingroup, conformity is much higher than in Asch's original study.

◆ Transmitting and Interpreting Messages

In this section, we discuss how Japanese and North Americans transmit and interpret verbal messages. We begin by looking at differences in communicator style. Next, we examine predispositions toward verbal behavior. Following this, we look at the recognition and expression of emotions. We conclude this section by examining how conflict is managed.

COMMUNICATOR STYLE

People perceive not only the content of verbal and nonverbal cues, but also the way the cues are communicated. The latter provides information concerning how the former is to be interpreted. Norton (1978) refers to the way the content is communicated as communicator style. More specifically, he defines this construct as "the way one verbally and paraverbally interacts to signal how literal meaning should be taken, interpreted, or understood" (1978, p. 99). In comparison to Japanese, North Americans are more attentive, contentious, and animated; they also leave a stronger impression and have stronger communicator images than the Japanese. The Japanese, in contrast, are higher than North Americans on the dramatic, open, and relaxed dimensions (Klopf & Cambra, 1981). These findings appear to be consistent with Hofstede's (1980) dimensions of cultural variability. Specifically, it would be expected that members of high uncertainty avoidance cultures (Japan) are more open and dramatic than members of low uncertainty avoidance cultures (United States). It also would be predicted that members of individualistic cultures are more attentive to verbal communication, be more contentious, leave stronger impressions based on verbal communication, and present a stronger communicator image than members of collectivistic cultures.

With respect to interpersonal criticism, both Japanese and North Americans prefer to express dissatisfaction in a direct way (Nomura & Barnlund, 1983). North Americans, however, use "active" forms of criticism (e.g., express dissatisfaction by making "constructive suggestions"), whereas Japanese prefer "passive" forms of criticism (e.g., express dissatisfaction nonverbally or ambiguously). The relationship individuals have with others influences the type of criticism used in Japan (i.e., the closer the relationship, the more "active" the criticism), but not in the United States. There are cultural differences in the management of compliments in Japan and the United States. Japanese prefer to express admiration nonverbally, by commenting on their own limitations, or by keeping their opinions to themselves.

North Americans prefer to direct their admiration to a third person, keep it to themselves, or express it nonverbally (Barnlund & Araki, 1985).[7] Both Japanese and North Americans prefer to apologize directly, but Japanese tend not to explain their behavior whereas North Americans tend to offer explanations. Japanese also use a wider range of apology strategies and adapt their strategies more to their partner's status than North Americans (Barnlund & Yoshioka, 1990).

There also are differences in how Japanese and North Americans respond to embarrassing situations in work settings. North Americans use justification, statements of fact, humor, and aggression more than Japanese (Sueda & Wiseman, 1992). North Americans also use humor as a coping strategy in embarrassing predicaments more than the Japanese, whereas Japanese use remediation (e.g., trying to fix the embarrassing situation) more than North Americans (Imahori & Cupach, 1991).

PREDISPOSITIONS TOWARD VERBAL BEHAVIOR

Cultural variation in uncertainty avoidance influences the degree of social anxiety individuals experience; the greater the uncertainty avoidance in a culture, the more individuals within the culture experience anxiety when communicating. Consistent with this prediction, Japanese and Koreans report higher levels of social anxiety than North Americans (Gudykunst, Yang, & Nishida, 1987). This is consistent with cross-cultural studies of communication apprehension (i.e., fear or anxiety associated with verbal communication; see Klopf, 1984).[8] Recognizing that Japanese and Koreans report higher levels of communication apprehension than North Americans should not be interpreted as implying that communication apprehension is a problem in Japan or Korea. In fact, the opposite is true: it is valued. Elliot, Scott, Jensen, and McDonald (1982), for example, argue that Koreans are attracted more to individuals who do not engage in a lot of verbal activity than they are to those who engage in high levels of verbal activity. A similar argument can be made for Japan. To illustrate, Okabe (1983) contends that Japanese see verbal communication as a means of communication, not the only means of communication. The concept of *enryo* (feelings of constraint or reserve) can be used to explain these patterns (see Chapter 2).

North Americans are more dominant, speak more frequently and longer, initiate conversations and maintain them more, are more inclined to talk, and are more fluent than Japanese (Cambra, Ishii, & Klopf, 1978).[9] Japanese also are less assertive and responsive than North Americans (Ishii, Thompson, & Klopf, 1990). Patridge and Shibano (1991) nevertheless argue that Japanese do behave assertively. Japanese assertiveness, however, takes place within the situational contexts in which they embed their behavior. Further, Japanese are less argumentive than North Americans (Prunty, Klopf, & Ishii, 1990). North Americans use feelings and emotions as information in verbal exchanges more than Japanese (Frymier, Klopf, & Ishii, 1990). Finally, North Americans are more immediate than Japanese (Boyer, Thompson, Klopf, & Ishii, 1990).

Predispositions toward verbal behaviors in the United States and Japan are consistent with cultural differences in individualism-collectivism.[10] Okabe (1983), for example, argues that people in individualistic cultures like the United States use an *erabi* (selective) worldview. With respect to verbal communication, they believe that "the speaker consciously constructs his or her message for the purpose of persuading and producing attitude change" (p. 36). People in collectivistic cultures like Japan, in contrast, hold an *awase* (adjustive) world view. With respect to verbal messages, they believe that a speaker should attempt "to adjust himself or herself to the feelings of his or her listener" (pp. 36-37).[11] Miyanaga (1991) contends that "to the Japanese, to be quiet and to listen is active, not passive" (p. 96).

In individualistic cultures self-esteem comes from the individual's being a dynamic agent and mastering his of her environment. In collectivistic cultures self-esteem emerges from the individual's adjusting herself or himself to the members of her or his ingroup.[12] Given the Japanese (collectivistic) concern for adjusting to others when communicating, it would be expected that they would engage in less domination of conversations, argumentativeness, aggression, and assertiveness than the individualistic North Americans, who are concerned with influencing others.

RECOGNITION AND EXPRESSION OF EMOTIONS

Darwin's (1872) evolutionary-genetic theory predicts that the expression of emotions is innate and universal. Extensive research has been conducted to test this hypothesis (see Gudykunst & Ting-Toomey, 1988, for a summary). Our focus here involves only comparisons including Japan and the United States.

There is high agreement between people in the United States and Japan when they classify photographs of facial expressions into one of eight categories of emotions: interest-excitement, enjoyment-joy, surprise-startle, distress-anguish, disgust-contempt, anger-rage, shame-humiliation, and fear-terror (Izard, 1968). Disgust and contempt can be recognized as different and correctly identified in Japan and the United States (Izard, 1970). Japanese understand the meaning of the emotion of joy the best and the meaning of shame the least; they dread disgust-contempt the most (Izard, 1970).

Agreement on labeling fundamental emotions is not limited to conditions in which observers are required to select only one emotion for each facial expression (Ekman et al., 1987). There is agreement in the United States and Japan on which emotion is strongest and which emotion is second strongest. Japanese also are as accurate at decoding vocal emotional expressions as students in the United States when they are provided sufficiently long samples of vocal communication (Beier & Zautra, 1972).

There are a large number of mood categories with equivalent Japanese and English markers, and Japanese and North Americans tend to agree on the "positive" and "negative" affect associated with mood categories (Watson, Clark, & Tellegen, 1984). One exception involves the category "sleepy." "Sleepy" has a negative connotation in the United States, but not in Japan. There are also several mood terms in English that are not well represented in Japanese (i.e., contempt, shyness, fear, blameworthiness, rage, pride, torment) and several Japanese terms not well-represented in English (i.e., nostalgia, irritability, reluctance, general unpleasantness, pain).[13]

The most recent emotion experienced by Japanese and North Americans is the same: disgust is experienced more recently than joy, anger, shame, or guilt, and these emotions are experienced equally and more recently than fear or sadness (Matsumoto, Kudoh, Scherer, & Wallbott, 1988). The North Americans, however, report experiencing emotions longer and with more intensity than the Japanese. Japanese and North Americans expect to experience the same emotions: they expect to experience joy and guilt more than fear, anger, sadness, disgust, or shame, which are expected to occur with equal frequency. Further, the relative pleasantness of the emotions is the same: joy is perceived as more pleasant than fear, shame, or guilt, which are perceived to be equally unpleasant but less unpleasant than anger, disgust, or sadness. Emotion-eliciting events have a more positive effect on the self-esteem and self-confidence of the North Americans than the Japanese. North Americans also report more bodily symptoms than Japanese when experiencing emotions. Japanese, in contrast, are more likely than North Americans to report that no action is necessary to cope with emotional experiences.

FACE NEGOTIATION AND CONFLICT RESOLUTION

"Face" involves the projected image of one's self in a relational situation. More specifically, face is conceptualized as the interaction between the degree of threats or considerations a member offers to another party and the degree of claim for a sense of self-respect (or the demand of respect) by the other party in a given situation (Ting-Toomey, 1985, 1988a).[14]

There are similarities and differences in the way Japanese and North Americans define face when interviewed in English

(Cole, 1989). Japanese definitions include honor, pride, claimed self-image, trustworthiness, individual standing or rank, politeness, respect extended by others, considerateness, and dignity. North American definitions include credibility, individual reputation, self-respect, ego, claimed position in interaction, appearance of strength, recognized positive worth, pride, status, lack of embarrassment, and self-defense. Japanese perceive that they lose face when they are not able to maintain ingroup harmony (e.g., when they shame or disgrace a friend or coworker). North Americans, in contrast, perceive they lose face when they personally fail (e.g., lose an argument). Japanese view insults or criticisms and rude or inconsiderate behavior from others as face threats, whereas North Americans see threats to their credibility or self-image as face threats. Both groups, however, agree that a face threat requires some self-protective action. Japanese see allowing others to look good or take a prestigious position as giving face. North Americans, in comparison, do not associate any particular behaviors with giving face. There also are differences in the situations individuals think maintaining self-face is important. Japanese want to preserve self-face in private, informal, and intimate situations. North Americans, in contrast, want to maintain self-face in public, formal, and nonintimate settings.

Ting-Toomey (1988a) contends that members of individualistic cultures like the United States express more self-face maintenance than members of collectivistic cultures like Japan. Members of collectivistic cultures, in comparison, express greater mutual-face and other-face maintenance than members of individualistic cultures.

With respect to conflict resolution styles, Ting-Toomey (1988a) argues that members of individualistic cultures like the United States use dominating, integrating, and compromising styles more than members of collectivistic cultures like Japan. Members of collectivistic cultures, in contrast, use avoiding and obliging conflict resolution styles more than members of individualistic cultures. North Americans use the dominating, integrating, and compromising conflict styles more than Japanese,

whereas Japanese use the avoiding conflict styles more than
North Americans (Ting-Toomey, Trubisky, & Nishida, 1989).[15]
Japanese also value public face in conflict situations and prefer
a collaborative style. North Americans, in contrast, prefer a compromising style (Cushman & King, 1985). Japanese use "passive"
accommodating styles when criticized, whereas North Americans prefer "active" confrontational styles (Nomura & Barnlund,
1983).[16]

◆ Communication in Japanese/North American Intercultural Relationships

There has been relatively little research on communication
in Japanese/North American relationships. In this section, we
summarize the limited research that has been conducted. We
describe how relationships develop by contrasting acquaintance
relationships, friendships, and romantic relationships. Next,
we discuss factors that contribute to effectiveness and satisfaction in Japanese/North American relationships.

RELATIONSHIP DEVELOPMENT

Individuals in close relationships engage in greater self-disclosure, ask more questions, share more networks, communicate more frequently, and have less uncertainty than individuals
in low-intimacy dyads (Gudykunst, Nishida, & Chua, 1986). Self-
disclosure, question asking, amount of communication, length
of relationship, and shared networks help reduce uncertainty
about others' values, attitudes, and beliefs across relationships.
Second language competence is associated with self-disclosure,
question asking, and the ability to reduce uncertainty. Individuals in close relationships also engage in more personalized and synchronized communication, but have less difficulty in communication than individuals in low-intimacy dyads
(Gudykunst, Nishida, & Chua, 1987). Second language compe-

tence clearly facilitates social penetration in Japanese/North American relationships.

Linguistic and cultural knowledge, empathy, and accommodation are rare in low-intimacy dyads, but are prominent in high-intimacy dyads (Sudweeks, Gudykunst, Ting-Toomey, & Nishida, 1990; Kertamus, Gudykunst, & Nishida, 1991). Background/lifestyle or similarity in attitudes and values is not recognized in low-intimacy dyads, but many similarities are noted in the high-intimacy dyads. Further, lack of cultural similarity is reported as a problem in low-intimacy dyads but is a positive factor in high-intimacy dyads. There is little involvement (amount and intimacy of interaction, and shared networks) in low-intimacy relationships, whereas partners in high-intimacy dyads characterize their relationships as having high levels of involvement.

With respect to opposite-sex relationships, partners in acquaintance relationships are viewed as relatively typical of their culture, whereas partners in friend and romantic relationships are seen as somewhat atypical members of their culture (Gudykunst, Gao, Sudweeks, Ting-Toomey, & Nishida, 1991). In acquaintance relationships, the partners have an interest in each other's culture, but linguistic knowledge inhibits them from getting to know each other. In friend and romantic relationships, the partners have an interest in and knowledge of each other's culture, and there are few linguistic barriers to communication. There is only minimal understanding of the partner in the acquaintance relationships, whereas there is moderate understanding at the verbal level in the friend relationships. Only romantic partners report deep understanding at both verbal and nonverbal levels.

There is a relatively low level of awareness of cultural differences in the acquaintance relationships, there is some awareness of general cultural differences in the friendships, and cultural differences are noticed and evaluated positively in the romantic relationships. Similarity in attitudes and interests is not recognized in the acquaintance relationships, but many similarities are recognized in the friend and romantic relationships.

The small amount of time spent together limits the development of the acquaintance relationships. There is, in contrast, sufficient time spent together for the relationship to develop in friend and romantic relationships. Finally, there is little self-disclosure of intimate information in the acquaintance relationships, but there is some in the friendships, and there are high levels of self-disclosure in the romantic relationships.

When individuals first get to know someone in Japanese/North American relationships, there is a need for them to express their cultural identities. In low-intimacy relationships, cultural identity is managed as a problematic issue or not recognized as a factor influencing their communication. This is expressed through not knowing or using the other person's language, seeing cultural differences as problems, and not accommodating to the other's style of communication. In close relationships, in contrast, cultural identity is recognized, but not seen as problematic. Partners involved in close relationships know the other person as an individual and accommodate to the partner's personal and cultural communication style.

EFFECTIVENESS AND SATISFACTION

Perceived effectiveness is associated with self-disclosure, interrogation, attraction, and similarity, as well as the reduction of uncertainty (Gudykunst, Nishida, & Chua, 1986). Further, communication satisfaction is associated with self-disclosure, interrogation, attraction, similarity, effectiveness, and the ability to reduce uncertainty. Satisfaction and effectiveness are closely related (Gudykunst et al., 1986; Ting-Toomey & Gao, 1988).

Miyahira (1991) asked Japanese to describe their prototype of the "ideal" North American with whom they would like to communicate. This prototype is a person who is tolerant of silence, listens to others, is not too direct, keeps one's word, and does not dominate the conversation. The North Americans' prototype of an "ideal" Japanese with whom they would like to communicate is a person who has a good sense of humor, favors confrontations, is not overly polite, is expressive, and is not unduly self-conscious.

Notes

1. Lebra (1976) points out that there is a general stranger anxiety (*hitomishiri*) in Japan. Maeda's (1969) research suggests that this anxiety exists in "normal" adults.

2. It should be noted that at least one study suggests that North Americans prefer an indirect rhetorical style more than Japanese (Ting-Toomey, 1988b). The results of Ting-Toomey's study, however, may be due to cultural bias in the measure of rhetorical sensitivity used. The instrument does not include items that would tap indirect forms of communication used in Japan.

3. Nishida (1991) also looked at topics that would be discussed in the first 6-15 minutes and 16-30 minutes, but only the first 5 minutes are reported here.

4. There is other research on nonverbal communication in Japan that does not make direct comparisons with nonverbal communication in the United States, but we do not include it here. For general discussions, see Morsbach (1988a, 1988b).

5. See Gudykunst (1989) for a summary of this argument.

6. See also Simmons, Vom Kolke, and Shimuzu (1986) for a discussion of differences in the way romantic relationships are experienced in Japan and the United States. Thakerar and Iwawaki (1979) also found that females in Japan and the United States perceive the same male faces to be attractive.

7. See Daikuhara (1986) for another study of compliments in Japan and the United States.

8. See Klopf (1984) for a summary of other research comparing communication apprehension in Japan and the United States. One study is inconsistent with this general trend. Nishida (1988) found that communication apprehension in Japanese adults is not different from that of adults in the United States. The differences may be due to the different samples (i.e., college students versus "adults").

9. More recently, Geatz, Klopf, and Ishii (1990) found differences on only two of the dimensions (domination of conversations and general inclination to talk), with North Americans scoring higher than Japanese on both dimensions.

10. Although we attempt to explain these findings conceptually, we believe it is important to recognize that these studies all involve the administration of translated instruments substantially developed in the United States in Japan. Few, if any, of the studies address the issue of conceptual equivalence of meaning in interpreting the results or conceptually explain why the differences exist.

11. Reynolds (1976) makes a similar point with respect to how individuals attempt to change in therapy. He argues that people in the United States (individualists) engage in "activity directed toward changing objective reality,"

whereas people in Japan (collectivists) engage in "activity directed toward changing one's inner attitudes or attention to objective reality" (p. 110).

12. See Okabe (1983) and Tezuka (1992) for a more extensive discussion of *awase*. Tezuka points out that the adjustment that takes place is reciprocal: both communicators adjust to each other. She also suggests that *sunao* ("being upright, obedient and docile without a negative connotation" [p. 41]) is important to understanding Japanese communication. See Murase (1984) for a discussion of the concept.

13. Sato, Mauro, and Tucker (1990) found that there are four cognitive dimensions used for the appraisal of emotions in Japan and the United States: pleasantness, certainty, attentional activity, and coping ability.

14. See Tada (1958) and Pharr (1990) for discussions of face in Japan. Morisaki and Gudykunst (in press) argue that scholars in the United States use the concept of face differently than Chinese and Japanese scholars do. They argue that in Japan and China face is related to social identity, not personal identity. As scholars in the United States use the concept, in contrast, face is based on personal identity. This distinction has important implications for studying face in Japan and the United States and needs to be pursued in future research.

15. The prediction for "obliging" (i.e., that Japanese would be more obliging than North Americans) was not supported. See Ohbuchi and Kitinaga (1991) for an alternative discussion of the use of power in conflicts in Japan.

16. Kumagai and Strauss (1983) discovered similar patterns. The results of Ting-Toomey et al.'s (1989) study also are compatible with discussions of conflict in Japan contained in Krauss, Rohlen, and Steinhoff (1984). Further, their data are consistent with studies of privacy regulation (e.g., Baker & Gudykunst, 1990; Naotsuka & Sakamoto et al., 1981) and the expression of emotion (Matsumoto et al., 1988) discussed earlier. Other studies (e.g., Peterson & Shimada, 1978) indicate that mediation is the preferred method for resolving disputes in Japan.

5

Expectations for Japanese/ North American Communication

In the previous chapters, we indicated that we have expectations about how others are going to communicate. Sometimes we are highly aware of our expectations and sometimes we are not. In this chapter, we discuss expectations in more detail. We begin by examining the nature of expectations. We then look at specific sources of expectations for others' behavior, focusing on those sources that contribute to misinterpretations and misunderstandings when Japanese and North Americans communicate. We conclude this chapter by discussing the processes Japanese and North Americans use to explain each other's behavior.

◆ The Nature of Expectations

Expectations involve anticipations and predictions about how others will communicate. Expectations are derived from social norms, communication rules, and the characteristics (including group memberships like culture) associated with others. Expectations also emerge from intercultural attitudes and stereotypes.

EXPECTATIONS ARE CULTURALLY BASED

There is a "should" component to expectations. "People who interact develop expectations about each other's behavior, not only in the sense that they are able to predict the regularities, but also in the sense that they develop preferences about how others *should* behave under certain circumstances" (Jackson, 1964, p. 225). Culture provides guidelines for appropriate behavior and the expectations used in judging competent communication.

When people are communicating with other members of their culture they usually are not aware of the norms and communication rules guiding their behavior. Following the norm or rule does not require effort or conscious thought (i.e., people follow the norms and rules they learned as children). Violating a norm or rule, in contrast, requires effort and thought. People also become aware of the norms and rules guiding their behavior when the norms or rules are violated and the individuals do not have a "ready made" interpretation for the violation.

EVALUATING VIOLATIONS OF EXPECTATIONS

If one person violates another's expectations to a sufficient degree that the violation is recognized, the person recognizing the violation becomes aroused and has to assess the situation (Burgoon & Hale, 1988). Burgoon and Hale argue that the degree to which the other person provides rewards affects how individuals evaluate the violation and the person committing the act. As used here, rewards refer to the benefits obtained from interactions with the other person (e.g., status, affection). If the other person provides rewards, individuals tend to choose the most positive interpretation of violations; "for example, increased proximity during conversation may be taken as a sign of affiliation if committed by a high reward person but as a sign of aggressiveness if committed by a low reward person" (Burgoon & Hale, 1988, p. 63). According to Burgoon and Hale, "positively" evaluated violations of expectations have "positive" consequences for communication with violators (e.g., no misinterpre-

tations, increases in intimacy). "Negatively" evaluated violations, in contrast, generally lead to "negative" outcomes (e.g.,
misinterpretations, decreases in intimacy).

Stephan (1985) argues that people often believe their expectations have been fulfilled when they communicate with members of other groups, regardless of how the person behaves. He
suggests that individuals tend not to change their behavior
when others disconfirm their expectations. Stephan goes on to
point out that the

> affective consequences of confirmation or disconfirmation depend
> to a great degree on whether the expectancy is positive or negative.
> Confirmation of positive expectancies and disconfirmation of
> negative expectancies would be expected to elicit favorable
> affective responses to the behavior, such as pride and happiness.
> Disconfirmation of positive expectancies and confirmation of
> negative expectancies may lead to negative affect, such as sad-
> ness or low self-esteem or resentment and hostility directed
> toward the self or the holder of the expectancy. (p. 637)

As Burgoon and Hale point out, however, whether the other
person can provide rewards (e.g., affection, status) influences
how individuals interpret the confirmation or disconfirmation
of their expectations. It is important to keep in mind that
Japanese and North Americans may not see each other as able
to provide rewards when they communicate.

NEGATIVE INTERCULTURAL EXPECTATIONS

Communication with members of other cultures usually is
based on negative expectations. Research indicates, for example, that actual or anticipated interaction with a member of a
different culture leads to anxiety.[1] As indicated in Chapter 1,
Stephan and Stephan (1985) argue that people fear four types
of negative consequences when interacting with members of
other groups.

First, individuals fear negative consequences for their self-concepts. In interacting with members of other cultures, individuals

worry "about feeling incompetent, confused, and not in control. . . . [They] anticipate discomfort, frustration, and irritation due to the awkwardness of intergroup interactions" (Stephan & Stephan, 1985, p. 159). People also may fear that they will lose self-esteem, that their social identities will be threatened, and that they will feel guilty if they behave in ways that offend members of other cultures. Both Japanese and North Americans, for example, may fear feeling incompetent when speaking each other's language. They also may feel awkward communicating with a person from the other culture in their own language.

Second, individuals may fear that negative behavioral consequences will result from their communication with members of other cultures. They may feel that members of other cultures will exploit them, take advantage of them, or try to dominate them. Individuals also may worry about performing poorly in the presence of people from other cultures or worry that physical harm or verbal conflict will occur. Japanese, for example, often fear verbal conflict when communicating with North Americans.

Third, individuals fear negative evaluations by members of other cultures. They fear rejection, ridicule, disapproval, and being stereotyped negatively. These negative evaluations, in turn, can be seen as threats to their social identities, especially their cultural identity. Given the "Japan bashing" in the United States and the negative comments about the United States made by Japanese politicians in recent years, it is not surprising that Japanese and North Americans experience anxiety when they communicate.

Finally, individuals may fear negative evaluations by members of their ingroups. If they interact with people from another culture, members of their culture may disapprove. They may fear that "ingroup members will reject" them, "apply other sanctions," or identify them "with the outgroup" (Stephan & Stephan, 1985, p. 160). Japanese who totally adopt North American behavior patterns, for example, are perceived negatively by other Japanese.

The anxiety individuals experience when communicating with members of other cultures is largely unconscious. To be managed, it must be brought to a conscious level (i.e., individuals must become mindful). To understand people from other cultures, individuals must cognitively manage their anxiety. Thinking about the behavior in which people need to engage when communicating with members of other cultures can reduce anxiety about interacting with them (Janis & Mann, 1977). Further, by finding out as much as possible and forming accurate impressions of other cultures, one can reduce anxiety and negative expectations (Neuberg, 1989). Stephan and Stephan (1989) also argue that the less ethnocentric individuals are, and the more positive their stereotypes are, the less intergroup anxiety they experience. These issues are examined in the next section.

◆ Ethnocentrism and Stereotypes

ETHNOCENTRISM

Sumner (1940) defines ethnocentrism as "the view of things in which one's own group is the center of everything, and all others are scaled and rated with reference to it" (p. 13). According to Levine and Campbell (1972), there are two facets to ethnocentrism. One involves the orientation toward the ingroup. If individuals are highly ethnocentric, they see their ingroup as virtuous and superior and their ingroup values as universal (i.e., applying to everyone). The second facet of ethnocentrism involves the orientation toward outgroups. If individuals are highly ethnocentric, they see outgroups as contemptible and inferior, reject outgroups' values, blame outgroups for ingroup troubles, and try to maintain social distance from outgroups.

Ethnocentrism is the tendency to interpret and evaluate others' behavior using ingroup standards (usually the ingroup standards used are the cultural standards). This tendency is natural and unavoidable. Everyone is ethnocentric to some degree. Although it is possible to have a low degree of ethnocentrism, it is impossible to be nonethnocentric. Ethnocentrism leads people to view their ways of doing things as the natural and "right" ways of doing things. The major consequence of this in an intercultural context is that people tend to view their cultural way of doing things as "superior" to other cultural ways of doing things. In other words, ethnocentrism is a bias toward the culture that causes individuals to evaluate different patterns of behavior negatively rather than trying to understand them.

Cultural relativism is the opposite side of the coin to ethnocentrism. Being culturally relative involves recognizing that the behavior of members of other cultures can be understood only in the context of their culture. If individuals try to understand the behavior of members of other cultures using their own culture's standards, they will inevitably misinterpret the behavior. If individuals are very high in ethnocentrism, they are very low in cultural relativism; and if they are very low in ethnocentrism, they are very high in cultural relativism.

One of the consequences of ethnocentrism and cultural relativism is the way individuals talk to people from other cultures. The speed with which individuals talk or the accent they use may be varied in order to generate different feelings of distance between them and members of other cultures (i.e., to make the distance seem smaller or greater). The concept of "communicative distance" can be used to explain this linguistic diversity:

> A communicative distance cannot be measured directly. It is not even visible. But we can be sure of its presence when we hear certain words or expressions. In other words, our awareness of a communicative distance in the midst of a conversation depends to a large extent on certain linguistic devices that serve, from the speaker's point of view, to set up the communicative distance, or from the hearer's point of view, to let the hearer know that it has already been set up by the speaker. (Peng, 1974, p. 33)

Lukens (1978) expands this conceptualization of communicative distance to isolate what she calls ethnocentric speech. To begin, it is important to recognize that there are different levels of ethnocentrism and cultural relativism. We can isolate five positions on a continuum: (1) very low cultural relativism/very high ethnocentrism, (2) low cultural relativism/high ethnocentrism, (3) moderate cultural relativism/moderate ethnocentrism, (4) high cultural relativism/low ethnocentrism, and (5) very high cultural relativism/very low ethnocentrism.

The distance of disparagement involves very high levels of ethnocentrism and very low levels of cultural relativism. This distance reflects animosity of members of one culture toward members of another culture (Lukens, 1978). It arises when the two cultures are in competition for the same resources. This level is characterized by the use of pejorative expressions about the members of the other culture and the use of ethnophaulisms (i.e., name calling). Lukens indicates that at this distance imitation and mockery of speech styles are characteristic. The current economic competition between Japan and the United States often leads to this distance being established when Japanese and North Americans communicate.

The distance of avoidance is established in order to avoid or minimize contact with members of other cultures. One technique commonly used to accomplish this is the use of one's native language or dialect. "The emphasizing of an ethnic dialect and other linguistic differences between the in-group and outsiders may be purposefully used by in-group members to make themselves appear esoteric to the out-group thus lessening the likelihood for interaction" (Lukens, 1978, p. 45). If Japanese and North Americans are communicating at this distance they might refuse to speak the other's language in everyday encounters.

The distance of indifference is the speech form used to "reflect the view that one's own [culture] is the center of everything" (Lukens, 1978, p. 42). This distance, therefore, reflects an insensitivity to other culture's perspectives. One example of the speech used at this distance is "foreigner talk," the form of speech used when talking to people who are not native speakers of a language. It usually takes the form of loud and slow speech patterns, exaggerated pronunciation, and simplification (e.g., deletion of articles). "We tend to believe that, if we speak slowly enough or loudly enough, anyone can understand us. I have done this myself quite without realizing it, and others have tried to reach me in the same way in Japanese, Chinese, Thai, Punjabi, Navajo, Spanish, Tibetan, and Singhalese" (Downs, 1971, p. 19). We discussed foreigner talk in Japanese/North American encounters in Chapter 3.

Gudykunst and Kim (1984) argue that the distance of sensitivity reveals a sensitivity to cultural differences. Speech at this level reflects the desire to decrease the communicative distance between the two cultures. When speaking at this level, members of one culture, for example, would adapt their communication behavior to members of the other culture. North Americans, for example, might avoid asking direct questions of Japanese.

The distance of equality reflects the desire to minimize the communicative distance between two cultures. This distance involves an attitude of equality, one where individuals demonstrate that they are interpreting the language and behavior of members of other cultures in terms of the other culture's standards. Speech at this distance avoids evaluations of the other culture.

The way individuals talk about people from other cultures is, in large part, a function of how they want to be seen by members of their own culture. van Dijk (1984) points out that

> people "adapt" their discourse to the rules and constraints of interaction and communication social settings. Especially when delicate topics, such as "foreigners," are concerned, social members will strategically try to realize both the aims of positive self-presentation and those of effective persuasion. Both aims, however, derive from the position of social members within their group. Positive self-presentation is not just a defense mechanism of individuals as persons, but also as respected, accepted, and integrated social members of [their culture]. And the same holds for the persuasive nature of [ethnocentric] talk; people do not merely lodge personal complaints or uneasiness about people of other [cultures], but intend to have their experiences, their evaluations, their opinions, their attitudes, and their actions shared by other members of [their culture]. (p. 154)

Everyone engages in ethnocentric talk to some degree. It is inevitable. Individuals can, however, reduce the degree to which they engage in ethnocentric talk if they are mindful of their communication.

STEREOTYPES

Stereotypes result from social categorizations. They are the "pictures" individuals have for the various social categories they use. Hewstone and Brown (1986) argue that stereotyping involves categorizing individuals, ascribing a set of traits to most or all of the members of that category, and applying these characteristics to individual members of the category. Like ethnocentrism, stereotyping is a natural result of the communication process. Individuals cannot not stereotype.

Stereotypes provide the content of individuals' social categories. Individuals have social categories in which they place people, and it is their stereotype that tells them what people in that category are like. We can draw at least four generalizations about the stereotyping process (Hewstone & Giles, 1986). First, stereotyping is the result of the tendency to overestimate the degree of association between group membership and psychological attributes. Although there may be some association between group membership and psychological characteristics of members, it is much smaller than individuals assume when they communicate on automatic pilot. Only 28-37% of the people in a culture have the traits attributed to them (Wallace, 1952). Also, in some cases there is more similarity in people based on their occupations across cultures than there is between occupations within a culture (Inkeles, 1974).

Second, stereotypes influence the way individuals process information. People remember more favorable information about their ingroups and more unfavorable information about outgroups. This, in turn, affects the way they interpret incoming messages from members of ingroups and outgroups. If Japanese and North Americans have negative stereotypes about each other, they will interpret messages from members of the other culture negatively.

Third, stereotypes create expectations regarding how members of other groups will behave. Stereotypes are activated automatically when individuals have contact with members of other cultures (Devine, 1989). Unconsciously, people assume that their expectations are correct and behave as though they are. Individuals, therefore, try to confirm their expectations when they communicate with members of other cultures.

Fourth, stereotypes constrain others' patterns of communication and engender stereotype-confirming communication. Stated differently, stereotypes create self-fulfilling prophecies. Individuals tend to see behavior that confirms their expectations, even when it is absent. They ignore disconfirming evidence when communicating on automatic pilot. If people assume someone else is not competent and communicate with him or her based on this assumption, he or she will appear incompetent (even if he or she is actually competent).

Japanese/North American stereotypes are learned from many different sources. They are based on past contact with people from the other culture, the mass media (television news and entertainment programs, movies), and books, among other sources. Some of the current stereotypes were presented in our introduction to Chapter 1.[2]

Many movies made in the United States are shown on Japanese television. In addition, several television dramas are presented (e.g., recent programs include "Murder, She Wrote" and "Miami Vice"). Japanese see North Americans as sociable, not shy, direct, relaxed, expressive, happy, interesting, energetic, powerful, friendly, strong, and confident (Fujioka, 1991). Japanese see themselves as inhibited, not confident, unexpressive, indirect, shy, sensitive, considerate, tense, and quiet. The more media from the United States that Japanese view, the greater the differences in their stereotypes of North Americans and Japanese.

North Americans' stereotypes of Japanese are based on numerous sources. For people who lived during World War II, many stereotypes are based on government propaganda disseminated during the war (see Johnson, 1991, for examples of stereotypes). Stereotypes also emerge from fictional books set in

Japan. James Michner's *Sayonara*, for example, provides a stereotype of Japanese women that still appears in current books and
movies (e.g., James Bond's escapades with Kissey Susuki in Ian
Fleming's *You Only Live Twice*). Other stereotypes of Japan
emerge from books like James Clavell's *Shogun* (which was a
major television miniseries), and Eric von Lustbader's *The Ninja*
and *The Miko*. Operas like Puccini's *Madam Butterfly* also
contribute to the stereotypes of Japanese.

Johnson (1991) argues that many North Americans tend to
have one global stereotype of "Asians" and that Japanese are
included in this stereotype. "This stereotype would include
certain physical features—slanted, almond-shaped eyes, black
straight hair, olive complexion, short stature—and certain personality and cultural traits—Asians are soft-spoken, sometimes
evasive, polite, quiet, reserved, family-oriented, hard-working"
(p. 164). She goes on to point out that

> the generalized Asian stereotype also comes in positive and negative
> versions, depending on how the United States feels about a particu-
> lar nation at a given time. When Americans were at war with
> Japan, quietness turned into deviousness, and stoicism . . . be-
> came cruelty. When Americans were fighting the Chinese in
> Korea, the same negative attributes were attached to them, whereas
> the Japanese suddenly became our trustworthy, hard-working,
> gentle allies. (p. 165)

Johnson contends that the images that individual members of
a culture have about people in another culture are a function
of the relation between the nations. Given the current tensions
between Japan and the United States, it would therefore be
expected that negative stereotypes of Japanese would prevail
in the United States.

Stereotypes, in and of themselves, do not lead to miscommunication or communication breakdown. If, however, simple or
negative stereotypes are held rigidly, they lead to inaccurate
predictions of the behavior of members of other cultures, and
misunderstandings occur. In order to increase effectiveness in
communicating with members of other cultures, individuals

need to increase the complexity of their stereotypes and question their unconscious assumption that most, or all, members of a culture fit a single stereotype (Stephan & Rosenfield, 1982).

Devine (1989) argues that conscious control of our reactions when our stereotypes are activated is necessary to control our ethnocentrism: "[Low ethnocentric] responses are . . . a function of intentional controlled processes and require a conscious decision to behave in a [low ethnocentric] fashion. In addition, new responses must be learned and well practiced before they can serve as competitive responses to the automatically activated stereotype-congruent response" (p. 15). This position is consistent with Langer's notion that mindfulness is necessary to reduce biases toward members of other cultures.

◆ The Attribution Process

ATTRIBUTIONS

People act as "naive" or "intuitive" scientists when they are trying to make sense of the world (Heider, 1958). Individuals are motivated by practical concerns such as their need to simplify and comprehend their environment and to predict others' behavior. Individuals use others' motives most frequently in explaining others' behavior. Heider points out that it is not experiences but individuals' interpretations of their experiences that constitute their "reality."

When group membership or culture is taken into consideration, the process is called social attribution. Social attributions are explanations that members of social groups, including cultures, use to understand the behavior of their own members and members of other social groups. Hewstone and Jaspars (1984) argue that attributions are social because (1) they are created in social interaction, (2) individuals use group membership as a way to explain others' behavior, and (3) people in a culture share a common way of making attributions. Hewstone and Jaspars argue that we enhance our social identities (including cultural identities) when we make social attributions. They also point out that our social attributions usually are based on the social stereotypes we share with other members of our culture. Our social attributions, however, can also be based on ethnocentrism.

Hewstone and Brown (1986) argue that when individuals perceive themselves and others in individual terms (e.g., their personal identities generate their behavior) or see an outgroup member as atypical, they tend to make person-based attributions. Person-based attributions, in turn, lead individuals to look for personal similarities and differences between them and the other person. When individuals perceive themselves and others as members of groups (e.g., their social/cultural identities generate their behavior), they tend to make category-based attributions. Category-based attributions then lead them to look for differences between their culture and the other culture.

ATTRIBUTION ERRORS

Several biases affect attributional processes. First, individuals have a tendency to overestimate the influence of personal, dispositional characteristics and underestimate the influence of situational factors when they make attributions (Kelley, 1967). This has been labeled the "fundamental attribution error" (Ross, 1977). Second, individuals tend to see their own behavior as normal and appropriate (the "egocentric" bias). They therefore explain others' behavior that is different as a function of their personal dispositions. When the people come from other cultures, individuals often use others' cultural background to explain their behavior. This involves an ethnocentric bias. Third, individuals tend to attribute their successes to personal disposition and their failures to situational factors (the "ego-protective" bias). Fourth, individuals stop looking for explanations for others' behavior once an acceptable explanation is found. Finally, individuals have a tendency to overemphasize negative information about others. This is referred to as the principle of negativity.

Pettigrew (1979) proposes that the "ultimate" attribution error is "a systematic patterning of intergroup misattributions shaped in part by prejudice" (p. 464). He points out that individuals' tendencies to attribute behavior to dispositional characteristics is enhanced when a member of another culture is perceived to engage in negative behavior. When members of another culture engage in what is perceived to be positive behavior, in contrast, the tendency is to treat the person as an "exception to the rule" and discount dispositional explanations for the behavior. Individuals therefore attribute the behavior to situational factors. It is very likely that individuals will make the ultimate attribution error when communicating on automatic pilot. To reduce the possibility of making this error when making attributions about the behavior of people from other cultures, individuals must be mindful of their interpretations of others' behavior.

MISATTRIBUTIONS IN JAPANESE/ NORTH AMERICAN COMMUNICATION

An example of how cultural differences in individualism-collectivism can lead to misunderstanding involves how face is negotiated. As indicated in the previous chapter, face is the public self-image individuals present to others (Ting-Toomey, 1988a). Individuals can have a concern for their own face or a concern for another's face. Problems in communication may occur when there is a difference in interpretation of the face-concern being used. In Japan, the concern for face is predominately other-oriented. In the United States, the concern is self-oriented. Misunderstandings may occur when North Americans fail to give face to Japanese when they interact.

Brislin, Cushner, Cherrie, and Yong (1986) present an example of this in the context of business negotiations between individuals in Japan and the United States:

> Phil Downing . . . was involved in the setting up of a branch of his company that was merging with an existing Japanese counterpart. He seemed to get along very well with the executive colleagues

assigned to work with him, one of whom had recently been elected chairman of the board when his grandfather retired. Over several weeks discussion, they had generally laid out some working policies and agreed on strategies that would bring new directions needed for development. Several days later . . . the young chairman's grandfather happened to drop in. He began to comment on how the company had been formed and had been built up by the traditional practices, talking about some of the policies the young executives had recently discarded. Phil expected the new chairman to explain some of the new innovative and developmental policies they had both agreed upon. However, the young man said nothing; instead, he just nodded and agreed with his grandfather. Phil was bewildered and frustrated . . . and he started to protest. The atmosphere in the room became immediately tense. . . . A week later the Japanese company withdrew from the negotiations. (pp. 155-156)

The young chairman of the Japanese company was giving his grandfather face by agreeing with him. This did not, however, negate any of the negotiations he had with Phil. Phil obviously did not understand this. By protesting and disagreeing with the grandfather, Phil not only failed to give face to the grandfather; he also threatened the grandfather's face. The young chairman therefore decided not to continue doing business with Phil.

Ehrenhaus (1983) argues that the types of attributions people make in individualistic and collectivistic cultures differ. Members of collectivistic cultures like Japan are sensitive to situational features and explanations and tend to attribute others' behavior to the context, situation, or other factors external to the individual. Members of individualistic cultures like the United States, in contrast, are sensitive to dispositional characteristics and tend to attribute others' behavior to characteristics internal to the individual (e.g., personality). This position is consistent with the use of self-serving biases in dealing with success and failure experiences in Japan and the United States (Kashima & Triandis, 1986).

Individuals use the information that they believe is important when interacting with members of other cultures. Because individuals' explanations are based on their own cultural presuppositions, there is a likelihood that misattributions will occur. North Americans, for example, will not emphasize situational factors enough when explaining the behavior of Japanese. Japanese, in contrast, will not emphasize intraindividual factors enough when trying to explain the behavior of North Americans.

Another area where misunderstandings may occur in communication between Japanese and North Americans is the directness of speech used. As indicated in Chapter 2, members of individualistic cultures like the United States tend to use a direct style of speech. Members of collectivistic cultures like Japan, in contrast, tend to use an indirect style of speech. The problem when people from individualistic and collectivistic cultures interact is illustrated in Tannen's (1979) study of Greek-North American communication. Although this study involves Greeks, Tannen's conclusion is applicable to Japanese/North American communication.

Tannen (1979) notes that Greeks tend to employ an indirect style of speech and interpret others' behavior based on the assumption that they also are using the same style. North Americans, in contrast, use a direct style of speech and assume others are using the same style. Tannen observes that when Greeks and North Americans communicate there often are misunderstandings due to these differences in style of speech. She goes on to point out that overcoming misunderstandings due to direct-indirect style differences is difficult because "in seeking to clarify, each speaker continues to use the very strategy that confused the other in the first place" (p. 5). To resolve the misunderstandings, obviously one of the people involved must recognize that the differences in styles are creating the problem, try to accurately interpret the other person's messages, and then shift her or his style of speech.

Misattributions also result from the way people in Japan and the United States try to reduce uncertainty, particularly in initial interactions with strangers. In the white, middle-class subculture in the United States, individuals try to obtain information about others' attitudes, feelings, and beliefs to reduce their uncertainty. In Japan, on the other hand, people must know others' status and background in order to reduce uncertainty[3] and know which version of the language to use (there are different ways to speak to people who are "superiors," "equals," and "inferiors"). This leads Japanese to introduce themselves saying things like "'I belong to Mitsubishi Bank' and immediately asking . . . 'What is your job?', 'How old are you?', and 'What is the name of your company?'" (Loveday, 1982, pp. 4-5). These questions are designed to gather the information necessary for a Japanese to communicate with a stranger. They are, however, perceived as "rude" and "nosey" by North Americans.

Notes

1. See Stephan and Stephan (1989) for several citations to support this claim.
2. See Yoshino (1992) for a discussion of how the *nihonjinron* view of Japanese is shared by the general population. This view creates a Japanese stereotype of the Japanese.
3. For a complete discussion of the cultural differences in how uncertainty is reduced, see Gudykunst and Ting-Toomey (1988).

6

Effective Japanese/
North American Communication

In Chapters 2, 3, and 4, we examined how culture, language, and communication are similar and different in Japan and the United States. In Chapter 5, we discussed how expectations influence Japanese/North American communication. Our purpose in this chapter is to integrate the material presented in these chapters and provide suggestions on how Japanese and North Americans can effectively communicate with each other.[1]

We organize this chapter around the characteristics associated with being perceived as competent communicators: motivation, knowledge, and skills (Spitzberg & Cupach, 1984). Motivation refers to the desire to communicate appropriately and effectively with others. Knowledge refers to awareness or understanding of what needs to be done in order to communicate appropriately and effectively. Skills involve abilities to engage in the behaviors necessary to communicate appropriately and effectively.

People may be highly motivated but lack the knowledge or the skills necessary to communicate appropriately and effectively. They also may be motivated and have the knowledge necessary, but not the skills. If people are motivated and have the knowledge and skills, this does not ensure that they will communicate appropriately or effectively. Several factors may intervene to affect their behavior. Individuals for example, may have a strong emotional reaction to something that happens and the emotional reaction may cause them to "act out" a script they learned earlier in life that is dysfunctional in the situation in which they find themselves. To illustrate, consider a North American who receives an indirect response to a direct question asked of a Japanese. He or she may have a strong negative reaction (e.g., become highly frustrated) to this type of response if he or she is not familiar with cultural differences in directness and indirectness. If the North American is unable to cognitively manage his or her emotional reaction, there is little chance that she or he will behave in a way that is effective in this situation.

It is also possible that individuals will act appropriately and effectively without actually having the knowledge necessary to engage in the behaviors by imitating the behavior of another person. Although this can work when communicating with someone from another culture when one does not have sufficient knowledge of the other person's culture, it is not the best strategy. As Wiemann and Kelly (1981) point out, "knowledge without skill is socially useless, and skill cannot be obtained without the cognitive ability to diagnose situational demands and constraints" (p. 290).

Individuals' motivation, knowledge, and skills interact with "outcomes" of their interactions with others to yield perceptions of competence. Two possible outcomes are that individuals' behavior may be perceived as appropriate and effective. Other potential outcomes include but are not limited to interpersonal attraction, trust, satisfaction with communication, the development of interpersonal relationships (i.e., intimacy), managing conflict, and adapting to other cultures. In the remainder of this chapter we isolate the components of motivation, knowledge, and skills that individuals can use to improve the quality of their Japanese/North American communication. Because this book is written in English and published in the United States, our focus is on what North Americans can do to communicate more effectively with Japanese. We begin with motivation.

◆ Motivation

As indicated earlier, motivation refers to the desire to communicate appropriately and effectively. In this section we examine four factors that influence motivation in Japanese/North American encounters. We begin by looking at the need for predictability. Next, we examine how the need to avoid diffuse anxiety affects motivation. Following this, we discuss how the need to sustain self-conceptions affects motivation. We conclude this section by examining the role of openness to new information in motivation.

NEED FOR PREDICTABILITY

One of the major reasons that Japanese and North Americans are not motivated to communicate with each other is that frequently the behavior of the people from the other culture is not predictable. Turner (1988) contends that individuals "need to 'trust' others in the sense that, for the purposes of a given interaction, others are 'reliable' and their responses 'predictable'" (p. 56). He goes on to point out that individuals have to feel that there is a "rhythm" to their interactions with others, and it is the predictability of others' behavior that provides this rhythm. When others' behavior is not predictable, individuals experience diffuse anxiety.

If individuals do not feel a part of interaction taking place, they will have a difficult time seeing others' behavior as predictable. One reason people may not feel part of the interaction is that Japanese and North Americans have learned different communication rules and often follow these rules when communicating in each other's language. If a Japanese follows his or her cultural norms regarding silence in conversations when speaking English, for example, North Americans will feel that the rhythm of the conversation is off, and they will not feel part of the conversation taking place.

If Japanese and North Americans do not recognize that predictability will be lower when they are getting to know a person

from the other culture, the low level of predictability will decrease their motivation to communicate. One way that individuals
can deal with this problem is to be mindful when they communicate with members of the other culture. When individuals are
mindful, they can gather information that will help them understand what is happening and therefore increase the predictability
of the other's behavior. We discuss gathering information later
in this chapter.

NEED TO AVOID DIFFUSE ANXIETY

Turner (1988) views anxiety as a "generalized or unspecified
sense of disequilibrium" (imbalance) (p. 61). Anxiety stems from
feeling uneasy, tense, worried, or apprehensive about what might
happen. It is an emotional (affective) response to situations
based on a fear of negative consequences (Stephan & Stephan,
1985). Turner argues that feelings of anxiety stem from depri-
vations in individuals' meeting their needs for security, predictability, group inclusion, and self-confirmation. He contends
that if individuals have not met their needs for security, predictability, and group inclusion, the focus of their behavior is on
trying to deal with the anxiety associated with not meeting
these needs. Because individuals are not highly aware of their
needs for security, predictability, and group inclusion, however,
they have a hard time pinpointing the source of the anxiety.
The net result is that "considerable interpersonal energy can be
devoted to meeting these needs as individuals grope around for
a solution to their often vague feelings of discomfort" (p. 63).

Anxiety is an important motivating factor in Japanese/North
American encounters. If anxiety is too high, Japanese and
North Americans will avoid communicating with each other or
cut their interactions short to lower their anxiety. To be motivated to communicate with each other, Japanese and North
Americans have to manage their anxiety if it is too high or too
low. This requires that they be mindful. We discuss the ability
to manage anxiety in the skills section. Another consequence

of high anxiety is that individuals' need to sustain their self-conceptions becomes important (Turner, 1988).

NEED TO SUSTAIN SELF-CONCEPTIONS

Self-conceptions influence how individuals communicate with others and the choices (conscious and unconscious) of those with whom they form relationships. Turner (1988) contends that individuals try to maintain their self-conceptions, and even go to the point of using defense mechanisms (e.g., denial) to maintain their views of themselves. Individuals' need for self-concept support directly influences their communication. Cushman, Valentinsen, and Dietrich (1982), for example, suggest that individuals are attracted to others who have the ability to support their self-concepts. Perceptions of each other's support of the other's self-concept is necessary if two people are going to form or maintain an interpersonal relationship.

One of the problems in Japanese/North American encounters is that one or both of the communicators perceives that the other person does not support his or her self-concept. If individuals are communicating on automatic pilot, they are likely to respond negatively in this situation. When individuals are mindful of their communication, however, they can recognize that Japanese and North Americans emphasize different aspects of their self-concepts. North Americans stress their personal identities, whereas Japanese emphasize their social identities. Failure to support each other's self-concepts, therefore, may not be due to a lack of concern, but rather to a failure to understand cultural differences in what the other considers to be important aspects of the self. To illustrate, Japanese are likely to ask questions about North Americans' social identities when North Americans expect questions about their personal identities. If North Americans perceive this as lack of self-concept support, they will not be motivated to interact with Japanese. If North Americans are mindful of their communication, however, they can recognize that this is just a cultural difference.

This interpretation should not have a negative effect on North Americans' motivation to communicate with Japanese.

OPENNESS TO NEW INFORMATION

Openness to new information involves the degree to which individuals willingly seek out new information. A personality characteristic that influences openness to new information is orientation toward uncertainty. Sorrentino and Short (1986) point out that

> there are many people who simply are not interested in finding out information about themselves or the world, who do not conduct causal searches, who could not care less about comparing themselves with others, and who "don't give a hoot" for resolving discrepancies or inconsistencies about the self. Indeed, such people (we call them certainty oriented) will go out of their way not to perform activities such as these (we call people who *do* go out of their way to do such things uncertainty oriented). (pp. 379-380)

Uncertainty-oriented people integrate new and old ideas and change their belief systems accordingly. They evaluate ideas and thoughts on their own merit and do not necessarily compare them with others. Uncertainty-oriented people want to understand themselves and their environment. Certainty-oriented people, in contrast, like to hold onto traditional beliefs and have a tendency to reject ideas that are different. Certainty-oriented people maintain a sense of self by *not* examining themselves or their behavior. Uncertainty-oriented people will recognize that their expectations for the behavior of members of other cultures are not necessarily accurate and are therefore more likely to try mindfully to reduce their explanatory uncertainty about others than are certainty-oriented people.

In Japanese/North American encounters, certainty-oriented people need to recognize mindfully that their tendency not to examine themselves or their behavior will lead to misunderstandings. People who tend to be certainty oriented can mindfully decide to examine their behavior when they are communicating with people from other cultures. If people are not open to new information about themselves and others, making accurate predictions and explanations of others' behavior is impossible.

◆ Knowledge

In this section we examine the knowledge component of perceived competence. We begin by looking at ways to gather information about members of other cultures. Following this, we focus on the role of knowledge about the other culture and its language in effective communication. Next, we examine the role of knowledge about similarities and differences and the role of positive expectations. We conclude this section with a discussion of the role of knowing more than one perspective in effective communication.

KNOWLEDGE OF HOW TO GATHER INFORMATION

Berger (1979) isolates three general types of strategies we can use to gather information about others and reduce our uncertainty about them and the way they will interact with us: passive, active, and interactive strategies. When individuals use passive strategies they take the role of "unobtrusive observers" (i.e., they do not intervene in the situation they are observing). Obviously, the type of situation in which they observe others influences the amount of information they gain. The first factor is the reactivity of the situation. If individuals observe others in a situation where they do not have to interact with others, the observers will not gain much information. Situations in which others are interacting with several people at once, in contrast, allow individuals to make comparisons of how the person being observed interacts with the different people.

The second factor that influences the amount of information available is the degree to which the situation inhibits individuals' behavior. If the situation is a formal one, others' behavior is likely to be a function of the roles they are filling in the situation, and the people doing the observation will not learn much about the person being observed as an individual. Informal situations where behavior is not guided by roles or social protocol, on the other hand, will provide useful information on others' behavior.

The active strategies for reducing uncertainty require individuals to do something to acquire information about others without actually interacting with them. One thing individuals can do to get information about others is to ask questions of someone who knows them. They also can gather cultural information about the other person by talking with a member of the other culture or a member of their culture familiar with the other culture. There are several concerns with using these strategies. First, the person being asked questions may tell the person about whom questions are being asked. Second, the person answering the questions may not give accurate information about the other person or the other person's culture. For North Americans to gather accurate information about Japan, for example, they must make sure that the other person is knowledgeable and not negatively biased against Japan.

The second active strategy is called environmental structuring. In using this strategy the person who wants to gather information does something to modify the other person's environment, observes the other person in the modified environment, and uses the other person's responses to gather information. This is the strategy that researchers use when they gather data in social science laboratories.

The interactive strategies of verbal interrogation (question asking) and self-disclosure are used when individuals interact with the person about whom they are trying to gather information.[2] One obvious way individuals can gather information about others is to use interrogation: that is, to ask them questions. There are limitations to this strategy that have to be kept in mind. First, only so many questions can be asked. Second, the questions must be appropriate to the nature of the interaction and the relationship with the other person. Third, the questions must be appropriate in the other person's culture.

It is the cultural appropriateness of the questions asked that often is most problematic in Japanese/North American interactions. As indicated in Chapter 4, Japanese and North Americans seek out different information to reduce uncertainty. If North Americans, for example, ask Japanese questions about their attitudes and values, they may not get direct answers because these questions are appropriate only in close relationships in Japan. To collect appropriate information when interacting with Japanese, North Americans need to ask group-based questions (see the "Ability to Adapt Behavior" section below).

The second way one can gather information about another person when interacting with her or him is through self-disclosure: telling the other person unknown information about oneself. Self-disclosure works as an information-gathering strategy because of the reciprocity norm (Gouldner, 1960). Essentially, the reciprocity norm states that if I do something for you, you will reciprocate and do something for me. The reciprocity norm appears to be a cultural universal; it exists in all cultures.[3] In conversations between people who are not close (i.e., people met for the first time, acquaintances), individuals tend to reciprocate and tell each other the same information about themselves that the other person tells them when interacting with a person from the same culture. If one person discloses his or her opinion on a topic when talking with someone, the other person will probably give her or his opinion on the same topic. The reciprocity norm may not operate in intercultural interactions when the information disclosed is inappropriate in the other culture. If a North American self-discloses to a Japanese and the Japanese does not reciprocate, probably the North American has found an area where self-disclosure norms differ.

KNOWLEDGE OF THE OTHER CULTURE

Some knowledge of the other person's culture is necessary for Japanese and North Americans to communicate effectively. It is not reasonable for North Americans to expect Japanese to understand their culture and totally adapt to communication patterns in the United States. For effective communication to occur, both communicators have a responsibility to try to understand each other's culture. The material presented in Chapters 2, 3, and 4 provides the foundation for Japanese and North Americans to make accurate predications and explanations of each other's behavior.

There are several important cultural differences between Japan and the United States that North Americans need to recognize in order to communicate effectively with Japanese. These include, but are not limited to, the following:

1. Japan is a collectivistic culture where people conceptualize themselves as interdependent with one another. This leads to an emphasis on *wa* in the ingroup, as well as an emphasis on *enryo* and *amae* in interactions with others. The importance of *wa* also leads to drawing a distinction between *tatemae* and *honne*.

2. High-context messages are used more frequently in Japan than low-context messages. This leads to an emphasis on indirect forms of communication as opposed to an emphasis on direct forms of communication in the United States. *Sasshi* is necessary to understand indirect messages.

3. Japan is a high uncertainty avoidance culture. This leads to an emphasis on rituals and the specification of relatively clear rules in most communication situations. People who deviate from the rules are viewed as dangerous and are therefore avoided whenever possible.

4. Japan is a high power distance culture. This leads to an emphasis on status (e.g., position, age) in communication. Power distance also leads to an emphasis on *on* and *giri* in relationships between individuals in Japan.

5. Japan is a highly masculine culture. This leads to an emphasis on communicating with members of the same sex and to separation of the sexes in many social situations.

These five conclusions are not all-inclusive, but they summarize how the major dimensions of cultural variability influence Japanese communication.

KNOWLEDGE OF
THE OTHER LANGUAGE

For communication to take place between Japanese and North Americans, at least one of the communicators must have some fluency in the other's language. The ideal situation would be for both communicators to be fluent in each other's language. The reason for this is that fluency in another person's language helps understand her or him when he or she speaks a second language. The ideal, however, is rarely met. Most frequently it is the Japanese who speaks English. If North Americans are in Japan, it is, nevertheless, important that they learn some Japanese. The more fluent North Americans are in Japanese, the more likely they will be able to accurately predict and explain Japanese behavior, even when the Japanese are speaking English.

KNOWLEDGE OF PERSONAL SIMILARITIES

Knowledge of the other's culture and language is not sufficient to communicate effectively and develop interpersonal relationships. To make accurate explanations and predictions of each other's behavior, North Americans and Japanese need to understand not only how their cultures and languages are similar and different, but also how they are similar as individuals. Usually when Japanese and North Americans first meet they focus on cultural differences. This is natural and to be expected. Langer (1989) points out that

> because most of us grow up and spend our time with people like ourselves, we tend to assume uniformities and commonalities. When confronted with someone who is clearly different in one specific way, we drop that assumption and look for differences. . . . The mindful curiosity generated by an encounter with someone who is different, which can lead to exaggerated perceptions of strangeness, can also bring us closer to that person if channeled differently. (p. 156)

Once individuals satisfy their curiosity about cultural differences, the search for individual commonalities and understanding can begin.

It is necessary to isolate differences before similarities can be recognized. If individuals first search for similarities and find some, they will generalize the assumption of similarity and be shocked when differences emerge. If individuals first recognize cultural differences and then search for individual commonalities, the probability of effective communication is increased. Bellah et al. (1985), for example, point out that individuals need to seek out commonalities because "with a more explicit understanding of what we have in common and the goals we seek to attain together, the differences between us that remain would be less threatening" (p. 287). Finding commonalities requires that individuals be mindful of their stereotypes and level of ethnocentrism. If North Americans hold their stereotypes of Japanese rigidly, for example, they will not see individual differences among the Japanese. This makes effective communication impossible.

Recognizing similarities between communicators is critical if a relationship is to develop between individual Japanese and North Americans. In Japanese and North American relationships, recognizing background similarities, lifestyle similarities, attitude similarities, and value similarities allows individuals to overcome cultural differences and develop close interpersonal relationships.

KNOWLEDGE OF MORE THAN ONE PERSPECTIVE

If individuals do not recognize that members of other cultures have a different perspective than they do, there is little chance of effective communication. At least three interrelated cognitive processes are involved when Japanese and North Americans try to make sense of each other's messages: description, interpretation, and evaluation. Description refers to an actual report of what is taken in through the senses with a minimum of distortion and without attributing social significance to the behavior. Interpretation involves attaching meaning or social significance to social stimuli. Evaluation involves judgment of social stimuli.

If individuals do not distinguish among the three cognitive processes, it is likely that they will skip the descriptive process and jump immediately to either interpretation or evaluation when communicating with members of other cultures. This is what communicators do when they are on automatic pilot. The problem is that individuals use their own cultural standards and rules for interpreting others' messages. This leads to misattributions of meaning and therefore to ineffective communication. If individuals mindfully distinguish among the three processes, on the other hand, they will be able to see alternative interpretations that are used by members of other cultures, thereby increasing the possibility of effective communication. Differentiating among the three processes also increases the likelihood of making accurate predictions and explanations of others' behavior.

To illustrate, consider eye contact behavior. If Japanese and North Americans are communicating, the North Americans will probably try to establish direct eye contact whereas the Japanese will tend to avoid it. If North Americans do not differentiate among description, interpretation, and evaluation, they will skip the description stage and interpret the behavior. Typical interpretations for lack of eye contact in the United States include that the other person is not telling the truth or is hiding something. These are likely to be inaccurate interpretations in Japan, where eye contact norms differ. If North Americans describe the behavior, they can search for alternative interpretations. Other interpretations might be that the person is shy, is showing respect, or generally does not engage in direct eye contact. Once alternative interpretations are isolated, North Americans can try to determine which is the most accurate interpretation of the Japanese behavior.

◆ Skills

In this section, we examine the behavioral skills necessary for effective Japanese/North American communication. We begin by looking at the ability to be mindful and the ability to tolerate ambiguity. Next, we examine the importance of the abilities to manage anxiety and to empathize. Following this, we discuss the abilities to adapt behavior and make accurate predictions.

ABILITY TO BE MINDFUL

By now it should be clear that we believe becoming mindful is an important aspect of communicating effectively with people from other cultures. Individuals must be cognitively aware of their communication if they are to overcome their tendency to interpret others' behavior based on their own frame of reference. Since we have discussed mindfulness at length throughout the book, we will not go into great detail here. There is, however, one point we want to reiterate. Namely, individuals are seldom highly mindful of their communication.

When North Americans interact with Japanese (and vice versa), they become somewhat mindful of their communication. The focus, however, is usually on the outcome ("Will I make a fool of myself?") rather than the process of communication. As you will recall from Chapter 1, focusing on the outcome does *not* facilitate effective communication. For effective communication to occur, the focus must be on the process of communication: that is, the interaction between the individuals.

Even when individuals communicate with people close to them, they are not mindful of the process. Csikszentmihalyi (1990) contends that "there are few things as enjoyable as freely sharing one's most secret feelings and thoughts with another person. Even though this sounds commonplace, it in fact requires concentrated attention [mindfulness], openness, and sensitivity. In practice, the degree of investment of psychic energy in a friendship is unfortunately rare" (p. 188). He goes on to argue that we must control our own lives if we want to improve our relationships with others. Such control requires that we be mindful.

If Japanese and North Americans are not mindful when they communicate, misunderstandings are inevitable because they will interpret each other's behavior from their own frame of reference. When Japanese and North Americans are mindful, they need to understand what the messages being exchanged mean from the other person's frame of reference. Effective communication can occur only when individuals understand each other's frame of reference.

ABILITY TO TOLERATE AMBIGUITY

Tolerance for ambiguity implies the ability to deal successfully with situations, even when a lot of information needed to interact effectively is unknown. More specifically,

> the ability to react to new and ambiguous situations with minimal discomfort has long been thought to be an important asset when adjusting to a new culture. . . . Excessive discomfort resulting from being placed in a new or different environment—or from finding the familiar environment altered in some critical ways—can lead to confusion, frustration, and interpersonal hostility. Some people seem better able to adapt well in new environments and adjust quickly to the demands of a changing milieu. (Ruben & Kealey, 1979, p. 19)

Ruben and Kealey suggest that people who have a higher tolerance for ambiguity are more effective in completing task assignments in other cultures than are people with lower tolerances. By extension, it can be argued that people who have a higher tolerance for ambiguity are more effective in communicating with members of other cultures than are those who have a low tolerance for ambiguity.

Individuals who have a low tolerance for ambiguity are likely to become frustrated in Japanese/North American encounters because of the ambiguity inherent in any intercultural interaction. If individuals know that they have a low tolerance for ambiguity, they can mindfully decide to accept the ambiguity present in Japanese/North American interactions. This in turn will decrease the likelihood that they will become frustrated when ambiguity occurs, and will increase the possibility of their communicating effectively.

ABILITY TO MANAGE ANXIETY

As indicated earlier, the amount of anxiety individuals experience when they communicate with members of other cultures influences their motivation to communicate. If anxiety is too high or too low, individuals will not be able to communicate effectively. If anxiety is too high, individuals will be preoccupied with managing their anxiety to communicate effectively. If it is too low, they will not have enough adrenaline flowing to want to communicate.

Kennerley (1990) isolates two general issues in managing anxiety: (1) controlling bodily symptoms, and (2) controlling worrying thoughts or cognitive distortions. There are several physical symptoms associated with anxiety. When individuals are highly anxious they may experience respiratory problems (e.g., difficulty in breathing), palpitations of the heart, dry mouth, muscular tension, or a tension headache.

To manage anxiety, Prather (1986) suggests the most important thing individuals can do is break away from the situation in which they feel anxious. This may mean excusing themselves to leave the room or mentally withdrawing for a short period of time. Once they have withdrawn, they need to calm themselves and remember that anxiety is not going to harm them. Individuals can allow their anxious feelings to pass and then return to the situation.

If anxiety does not dissipate quickly, individuals need to do something that will restore their calm. Individuals can use various techniques to control the physical symptoms associated with anxiety, including but not limited to yoga, hypnotism, meditation, and progressive muscular relaxation (i.e., relaxing the various muscle groups in one's body in a systematic fashion).

Respiratory control also can be used to manage the physical symptoms of anxiety. One way to practice controlled breathing is to sit up straight and concentrate on your breathing. Mindfully draw in a long breath and focus on your inhaling. Then let out the breath, focusing on your exhaling.

Individuals can control their worrying thoughts by overcoming their cognitive distortions. When individuals interpret their own and others' behavior, their perceptions often are distorted because of the ways they think about their feelings and behavior. Burns (1989) isolates 10 forms of cognitive distortions that influence the ways we interpret behavior: (1) all-or-nothing thinking, (2) making overgeneralizations, (3) using mental filters, (4) discounting the positive and focusing only on the negative, (5) jumping to conclusions, (6) magnification, or making problems bigger than they are, (7) using emotional reasoning, (8) using "should" statements (e.g., I should be a better person), (9) labeling, and (10) blaming ourselves or others. To overcome worrying thoughts, individuals need to be mindful of their communication. When individuals are mindful, they need to replace the worrying thoughts with rational responses. Unless individuals stop distorting their thought processes, they will *not* be able to manage their anxiety consistently over long periods of time.

Managing anxiety is critical for Japanese and North Americans to communicate effectively. If anxiety is too high or too low, individuals will not be motivated to communicate with each other. When anxiety is too high, individuals' cognitive processing is distorted by their worrying thoughts, and therefore they cannot understand the other person. In Japanese/North American interactions individuals' stereotypes of the other culture influence their interpretations of others' behavior when anxiety is high. This often leads to the use of overgeneralizations, magnification of problems, blaming, and so forth. When individuals mindfully manage their anxiety and try to understand the other person's perspective, they can overcome their cognitive distortions and improve the effectiveness of their communication.

ABILITY TO EMPATHIZE

Sympathy involves "the imaginative placing of ourselves in another person's position" (Bennett, 1979, p. 411). When individuals are sympathetic, they imagine how they would think or feel in the other person's situation. Empathy, in contrast, involves "the imaginative intellectual and emotional participation in another person's experience" (Bennett, 1979, p. 418). When individuals empathize, they imagine how the other person thinks or feels in the situation.

Bell (1987) points out that empathy is multifaceted, involving cognitive (thinking), affective (feeling), and communication components:

> Cognitively, the empathic person takes the perspective of the another person, and in so doing strives to see the world from the other's point of view. Affectively, the empathic person experiences the emotions of another; he or she *feels* the other's experiences. Communicatively, the empathic individual signals understanding and concern through verbal and nonverbal cues. (p. 204)

The cognitive, affective, and communication components are highly interrelated, and all must be present for others to perceive that we are being empathic.

Being empathic is one of the major characteristics associated with communication effectiveness across cultures (Hwang, Chase, & Kelly, 1980). Several characteristics appear to be associated with empathy: (1) "listening carefully to what people say," (2) understanding "how other people are feeling," (3) being "interested in what others have to say," (4) being "sensitive to the needs of other people," and (5) understanding "another's point of view" (Hwang, Chase, & Kelly, 1980, p. 74). Although these indicators of empathy include verbal components, individuals tend to rely on nonverbal behavior more than verbal behavior when they interpret others' behavior as empathic (Bell, 1987).

If Japanese and North Americans respond to each other with sympathy, misunderstandings are inevitable. To communicate effectively, developing the ability to empathize is necessary. Being empathic requires that individuals be mindful of their communication in Japanese/North American encounters.

ABILITY TO ADAPT BEHAVIOR

To gather appropriate information about strangers requires that we be able to adapt our behavior. Individuals also must be able to adapt and accommodate their behavior to the people from the other culture if they are going to be successful in their Japanese/North American interactions. Some scholars argue that flexibility in adapting behavior is the critical component of intercultural effectiveness.[4] Duran (1983) argues that communication adaptability involves: "1) The requirement of both cognitive (ability to perceive) and behavioral (ability to adapt) skills; 2) Adaptation not only of behaviors but also interaction goals; 3) The ability to adapt to the requirements posed by different communication contexts; and 4) The assumption that perceptions of communicative competence reside in the dyad" (p. 320).

Failure to adapt behavior frequently creates problems in Japanese/North American relationships. One area where problems emerge has to do with meeting obligations (*giri*). Christopher (1983), for example, argues that "a Japanese comes to expect more of an American acquaintance than the American is prepared to give—with the result that the Japanese is confused and sometimes embittered by the American's sudden, and to the Japanese way of thinking, inexplicable evasion of the unspoken obligations of their relationship" (p. 172).

There are several areas where North Americans might want to consider adapting their behavior when communicating with Japanese to increase effectiveness. Adaptations can be based on the cultural differences isolated in Chapter 2. We cannot discuss all of the adaptations North Americans might make. We provide a few suggestions for behavioral adaptation. Our purpose is *not* to suggest specific behaviors North Americans should use when communicating with Japanese. Individuals must consciously decide how to communicate in the specific situations in which they find themselves to be effective; they should *not* try to memorize a list of "dos and don'ts." The examples we present are designed only to illustrate potential areas of adaptation.

To begin, consider adaptations based on cultural differences in individualism-collectivism. Triandis, Brislin, and Hui (1988) provide broad suggestions for individualists to adapt their behavior when interacting with collectivists:[5] (1) understand collectivists' group memberships in order to predict their behavior; (2) recognize that when collectivists' group memberships change, their behavior changes too; (3) be prepared to establish vertical relationships with collectivists; (4) try to be cooperative with collectivists, since they will see competition as threatening; (5) try to establish harmonious relationships with collectivists; (6) avoid confrontation with collectivists when possible; (7) help collectivists maintain face (public self-image) in public; (8) recognize that collectivists do not separate criticism from the person being criticized; (9) recognize that collectivists value long-term relationships; (10) recognize that collectivists value modesty; (11) recognize that collectivists are more formal in initial interactions than individualists; (12) follow collectivists' lead in self-disclosure; and (13) try to understand collectivists' obligations to others.

Ting-Toomey (1994) provides similar suggestions for individualists to manage conflicts with collectivists.[6] First, individualists need to remember that collectivists use an interdependent self-construal. Their actions reflect on their ingroup and they have to take their ingroups into consideration in managing conflicts. Second, individualists should try to deal with conflicts when they are small rather than allow them to become large issues, and recognize that collectivists may want to use a third party to mediate the conflict. Third, individualists need to help the collectivists maintain face (public image) during the conflict. This means not humiliating or embarrassing collectivists in public. Fourth, individualists need to pay attention to collectivists' nonverbal behavior and pay attention to implicit messages.

Fifth, individualists need to actively listen when collectivists talk. Sixth, individualists need to use indirect messages more than they typically do. This means using qualifier words (e.g., maybe, possibly), being more tentative, and avoiding bluntly saying no. Seventh, Ting-Toomey suggests that individualists let go of conflict if collectivists do not want to deal with it (recall that avoiding is the preferred collectivist strategy).

Specific suggestions for behavioral adaptations in Japanese/North American interactions also can be made. North Americans, for example, might consider adapting the degree to which they indicate they are dependent on others when they communicate with Japanese. In the United States, individualism leads people to act as though they are totally independent of others. Collectivism in Japan, however, leads people to act and talk as though they are dependent on others. Not recognizing one's dependence on others "seems egotistical and ungrateful" to Japanese (Naotsuka & Sakamoto, 1981). North Americans, for example, can make explicit statements of their dependence on the Japanese with whom they develop relationships. The best way to determine the types of statements to make is to listen carefully to the statements that Japanese make to each other.

Also related to collectivism is the issue of self-assertion (individualism) and self-deprecation (collectivism). If North Americans are highly assertive when communicating with Japanese, the Japanese will probably feel uncomfortable because self-deprecation is the norm. When offering food, for example, a Japanese might say "This food is not delicious." North Americans do not necessarily have to go this far in self-deprecation, but avoiding self-assertion clearly will increase the likelihood of effective communication with Japanese.

Another area where North Americans might consider adapting their behavior involves the issue of directness and indirectness. If North Americans are highly direct with Japanese in either Japanese or English, it will inhibit communication effectiveness. North Americans can try to interpret indirect cues from Japanese in a Japanese cultural context and at the same time transmit messages that will not threaten the public image of Japanese. Adaptations in this area might also include apologizing in awkward situations more than is typical in the United States and avoiding direct confrontations with Japanese when possible. "Japanese feel that mutual apology [indicates] a willingness on the part of each party to consider the possibility of his [or her] own error. . . . [It] calms things down so that the relationship [can] function smoothly" (Naotsuka & Sakamoto, 1981, p. 167).

These examples are not all-inclusive, but they illustrate ways that North Americans can adapt their behavior when they are mindful in order to communicate more effectively with Japanese. Whatever adaptations are made, they must allow North Americans to sustain their self-conceptions. If North Americans adapt their behavior to the extent that it threatens their self-conceptions, it will *not* facilitate effective communication.

We are not suggesting that it is only the North Americans' responsibility to adapt their behavior. Japanese have an equal responsibility (we have focused on North American adaptations because this book is written in English). If each person takes responsibility for adapting behavior in ways with which he or she is comfortable, then the effectiveness of communication will increase. If one person does not adapt his or her behavior, however, it does not relieve the other person from her or his responsibility to adapt her or his behavior.

ABILITY TO MAKE ACCURATE PREDICTIONS

Reducing uncertainty and accurately predicting others' behavior requires that individuals be able to describe others' behavior and select accurate interpretations of their messages. To be able to accomplish these objectives, individuals must be able to gather appropriate information about members of other cultures. One of the problems in gathering the appropriate information in Japanese/North American encounters is that anxiety often is high. Wilder and Shapiro (1989) point out that when anxiety is too high individuals are not able to gather accurate information about others. Individuals therefore will not be able to make accurate predictions or explanations of others' behavior.

North Americans need to recognize that personal information about Japanese (e.g., their individual values and attitudes) will not be a good predictor of their behavior in most relationships (it is useful only in close friendships). They therefore need to seek out mindfully information about the Japanese that will help them understand the behavior of the individuals with whom they interact. North Americans, for example, need to gather information about Japanese group memberships, status, age, marital status, and so forth. Searching for background information is important because "failure to ask in detail about events in the other person's life (e.g., 'Are you married?', 'Why don't you have children?', 'Are you going to live with your husband's parents') would seem cold and unfriendly to a Japanese, indicating a lack of sympathy and an unwillingness to treat the other person as a friend" (Naotsuka & Sakamoto, 1981, p. 169).

Probably the most critical aspect of gathering appropriate information for North Americans when communicating with Japanese is learning to interpret indirect messages. If North Americans expect direct responses to the questions they ask Japanese, they will not be able to gather the information they need to reduce their uncertainty. Most indirect responses, however, can be interpreted accurately if North Americans understand the Japanese culture and take the relationship between the people and the context into consideration when interpreting the messages.

◆ Conclusion

Our purpose in writing this book was to help Japanese and North Americans communicate more effectively with each other. Encountering cultural differences in communication can be both a source of problems in communication and a source of personal growth. The problems often are similar to a novice student's first response to the Zen koan developed by Zen Master Haukin (1686-1769): "In clapping both hands a sound is heard; what is the sound of one hand?" Insight is necessary to grasp the answer to this koan. Insight also is necessary to communicate effectively in Japanese/North American encounters and to see the potential for personal growth in intercultural encounters. We hope that the material presented in the book provides insights that will help North Americans and Japanese communicate with each other in a way that is consistent with the Vulcan greeting on *Star Trek*: "Greetings! I am pleased to see that we are different. May we together become greater than the sum of both of us."

Notes

1. The suggestions presented in this chapter are based on Gudykunst's (1993) theory of effective interpersonal and intergroup communication. Not all of the factors isolated in the theory are discussed.

2. Berger also isolates a third interactive strategy, deception detection, not discussed here.

3. There are some differences in how it is manifested in different cultures. See Gudykunst and Ting-Toomey (1988) for a detailed discussion.

4. Michael Bond recently made this argument in a personal communication.

5. Not all of their suggestions are summarized here. They also give suggestions for collectivists interacting with individualists. These are omitted to conserve space. Most are the opposite of those provided here.

6. Ting-Toomey (1994) also provides suggestions for collectivists to manage conflict with individualists.

References

Akasu, K., & Asao, K. (1993). Sociolinguistic factors influencing communication in Japan and the United States. In W. B. Gudykunst (Ed.), *Communication in Japan and the United States*. Albany: State University of New York Press.

Allen, L. (1983). Review of *Japan's modern myth*. *Monumenticia Nipponica, 38*, 333-338.

Altman, I. (1977). Privacy: Culturally universal or culturally specific. *Journal of Social Issues, 33*, 66-84.

Altman, I., & Taylor, D. (1973). *Social penetration processes*. New York: Holt, Reinhart, and Winston.

Argyle, M., Henderson, M., Bond, M., Iizuka, Y., & Contarelo, A. (1986). Cross-cultural variations in relationship rules. *International Journal of Psychology, 21*, 287-315.

Asch, S. E. (1956). Studies of independence and conformity. *Psychological Monographs, 70*, No. 9 (whole No. 416).

Atsumi, R. (1980). Patterns of personal relationships: A key to understanding Japanese thought and behavior. *Social Analysis, 5/6*, 63-78.

Baker, J., & Gudykunst, W. B. (1990). *Privacy regulation in Japan and the United States*. Paper presented at the International Communication Association Convention, Dublin.

Ball-Rokeach, S. (1973). From pervasive ambiguity to definition of the situation. *Sociometry, 36*, 378-389.

Barnlund, D. (1975). *The public and private self in Japan and the United States*. Tokyo: Simul Press.

Barnlund, D. (1989). *Communicative styles of Japanese and Americans*. Belmont, CA: Wadsworth.

Barnlund, D., & Araki, S. (1985). Intercultural encounters: The management of compliments by Japanese and Americans. *Journal of Cross-Cultural Psychology, 16*, 9-27.

Barnlund, D., & Yoshioka, M. (1990). Apologies: Japanese and American styles. *International Journal of Intercultural Relations, 14*, 193-205.

Beck, A. (1988). *Love is never enough*. New York: Harper & Row.

Beebe, L., & Takahashi, T. (1989). Socioloinguistic variations in face threatening acts. In M. Eisenstein (Ed.), *The dynamic interlanguage*. New York: Plenum.

Befu, H. (1977). Power in the great white tower. In R. Fogelson & R. Adams (Eds.), *The anthropology of power*. New York: Academic Press.

Befu, H. (1980a). A critique of the group model of Japanese society. *Social Analysis, 5/6*, 29-43.

Befu, H. (1980b). The group model of Japanese society and an alternative. *Rice University Studies, 66*, 169-187.

Befu, H. (1986). Gift-giving in modernizing Japan. In T. Lebra & W. Lebra (Eds.), *Japanese culture and behavior* (rev ed.). Honolulu: University of Hawaii Press.

Beier, E., & Zautra, A. (1972). Identification of vocal components of emotions across cultures. *Journal of Consulting and Clinical Psychology, 34*, 166-175.

Bell, R. (1987). Social involvement. In J. McCroskey & J. Daly (Eds.), *Personality and interpersonal communication*. Newbury Park, CA: Sage.

Bellah, R., Madsen, R., Sullivan, W., Swidler, A., & Tipton, S. (1985). *Habits of the heart: Individualism and commitment in American life*. New York: Harper & Row.

Bennett, M. (1979). Overcoming the golden rule: Empathy and sympathy. In D. Nimmo (Ed.), *Communication yearbook 3*. New Brunswick, NJ: Transaction Books.

Berger, C. R. (1979). Beyond initial interaction. In H. Giles & R. St. Clair (Eds.). *Language and social psychology*. Oxford, UK: Basil Blackwell.

Berger, C. R., & Calabrese, R. (1975). Some explorations in initial interactions and beyond: Toward a developmental theory of interpersonal communication. *Human Communication Research, 1*, 99-112.

Berger, C. R., & Bradac, J. (1982). *Language and social knowledge*. London: Edward Arnold.

Berger, C. R., & Douglas, W. (1982). Thought and talk: "Excuse me, but have I been talking to myself?" In F. Dance (Ed.), *Human communication theory*. New York: Harper & Row.

Berger, C. R., Gardner, R. R., Parks, M. R., Schulman, L., & Miller, G. R. (1976). Interpersonal epistemology and interpersonal communication. In G. R. Miller (Ed.), *Explorations in interpersonal communication*. Beverly Hills, CA: Sage.

Bernstein, B. (1973). *Class, codes, and control* (Vol. 1). London: Routledge and Kegan Paul.

Boyer, L., Thompson, C., Klopf, D., & Ishii, S. (1990). An intercultural comparison of immediacy among Japanese and Americans. *Perceptual and Motor Skills, 71*, 65-66.

Brislin, R., Cushner, K., Cherrie, C., & Yong, M. (1986). *Intercultural interactions*. Beverly Hills, CA: Sage.

Burgoon, J., & Hale, J. (1988). Nonverbal expectancy violations. *Communication Monographs, 55*, 58-79.

Burns, D. (1989). *The feeling good handbook*. New York: William Morrow.

Cambra, R., Ishii, S., & Klopf, D. (1978). *Four studies of Japanese speech characteristics.* Paper presented at the Communication Association of the Pacific Convention, Tokyo.

Caudill, W., & Scarr, H. (1961). Japanese value orientations and culture change. *Ethnology, 1,* 53-91.

Chinese Culture Connection. (1987). Chinese values and the search for culture-free dimensions of culture. *Journal of Cross-Cultural Psychology, 18,* 143-164.

Christopher, R. (1983). *The Japanese mind.* New York: Simon & Schuster.

Cole, M. (1989). *A cross-cultural inquiry into the meaning of face in the Japanese and United States cultures.* Paper presented at the Speech Communication Association Convention, San Francisco.

Cole, M. (1990). *Relational distance and personality influences on conflict communication styles.* Paper presented at the Speech Communication Association convention, Chicago.

Condon, J. (1984). *With respect to the Japanese.* Yarmouth, ME: Intercultural Press.

Csikszentmihalyi, M. (1990). *Flow: The psychology of optimal experience.* New York: Harper & Row.

Cushman, D. P., & King, S. S. (1985). National and organizational cultures in conflict resolution: Japan, the United States, and Yugoslavia. In W. B. Gudykunst, L. P. Stewart, & S. Ting-Toomey (Eds.), *Communication, culture, and organizational processes.* Beverly Hills, CA: Sage.

Cushman, D., & Nishida, T. (1983). *Mate selection in Japan and the United States.* Unpublished paper, State University of New York, Albany.

Cushman, D., Valentinsen, B., & Dietrich, D. (1982). A rules theory of interpersonal relationships. In F. Dance (Ed.), *Human communication theory.* New York: Harper & Row.

Daikuhara, M. (1986). A study of compliments from a cross-cultural perspective: Japanese and American English. *Working Papers in Educational Linguistics, 2* (2), 103-135.

Dale, P. N. (1986). *The myth of Japanese uniqueness.* New York: St. Martin's Press.

Darwin, C. (1872). *The expression of emotions in man and animals.* London: John Murray.

Devine, P. (1989). Stereotypes and prejudice. *Journal of Personality and Social Psychology, 56,* 5-18.

DeVos, G. (1985). Dimensions of the self in Japanese culture. In A. Marsella, G. DeVos, & F. Hsu (Eds.), *Culture and self.* New York: Tavistock.

Doi, T. (1973). *The anatomy of dependence.* Tokyo: Kodansha.

Doi, T. (1986). *The anatomy of self.* Tokyo: Kodansha.

Dore, R. (1958). *City life in Japan.* Berkeley: University of California Press.

Downs, J. (1971). *Cultures in crisis.* Chicago: Glencoe.

Dulles, F. R. (1965). *Yankees and samurai.* New York: Harper & Row.

Duran, R. L. (1983). Communicative adaptability. *Communication Quarterly, 31,* 320-326.

Edgerton, R. B. (1985). *Rules, exceptions, and social order.* Berkeley: University of California Press.

Ehrenhaus, P. (1983). Culture and the attribution process: Barriers to effective communication. In W. B. Gudykunst (Ed.), *Intercultural communication theory.* Beverly Hills, CA: Sage.

Ekman, P., Friesen, W., O'Sullivan, M., Diacoyanni-Tarlatzis, I., Krause, R., Pitcairn, T., Scherer, K., Chan, A., Heider, K., Compte, W., Ricci-Bitti, P., Komita, M., & Tzavaras, A. (1987). Personality processes and individual differences: Universals and cultural differences in the judgments of facial expressions. *Journal of Personality and Social Psychology, 53,* 712-717.

Elliot, S., Scott, M., Jensen, A., & McDonald, M. (1982). Perceptions of reticence: A cross-cultural investigation. In M. Burgoon (Ed.), *Communication yearbook 5.* New Brunswick, NJ: Transaction Books.

Engebretson, D., & Fullmer, D. (1970). Cross-cultural differences in territoriality: Interaction differences of native Japanese, Hawaii Japanese, and American Caucasians. *Journal of Cross-Cultural Psychology, 1,* 261-269.

Ervin-Tripp, S. (1964). Interaction of language, topic and listener. *American Anthropologist, 66*(6), 86-102.

Fisher, B. A. (1978). *Perspectives on human communication.* New York: Macmillan.

Frager, R. (1970). Conformity and anticonformity in Japan. *Journal of Personality and Social Psychology, 15,* 203-210.

Friesen, W. (1972). *Cultural differences in facial expression in a social situation: An experimental test of the concept of display rules.* Unpublished Ph.D. dissertation, University of California, San Francisco.

Frymier, A., Klopf, D., & Ishii, S. (1990). Japanese and Americans compared on the affect orientation construct. *Psychological Reports, 66,* 985-986 (also published in *Communication Research Reports,* 1990, 7, 63-66).

Fujihara, T., & Kurokawa, M. (1981). *Taijinkankei ni okeru "amae" ni tsuiteno jisshoteki kenkyu* [An empirical study of *amae* (dependence) in interpersonal relations]. *Jikkenshakaishinrigigaku Kenkyu* [Japanese Journal of Experimental Social Psychology], 21, 53-62.

Fujioka, Y. (1991). *Impact of American mass media on Japanese interpersonal communication patterns.* Paper presented at the Conference on Communication in Japan and the United States, California State University, Fullerton.

Geatz, L., Klopf, D., & Ishii, S. (1990). *Predispositions toward verbal behavior of Japanese and Americans.* Paper presented at the Communication Association of Japan Convention, Tokyo.

Gass, S., & Varonis, E. (1984). The effect of familiarity on the comprehensibility of nonnative speech. *Language Learning, 34,* 65-89.

Giles, H., Coupland, N., & Wiemann, J. (1992). "Talk is cheap . . ." but "my word is my bond." In R. Bolton & H. Kwok (Eds.), *Sociolinguistics today.* London: Routledge.

Gouldner, A. (1960). The norm of reciprocity. *American Sociological Review, 25,* 161-179.

Gudykunst, W. B. (1987). Cross-cultural comparisons. In C. R. Berger & S. Chaffee (Eds.), *Handbook of communication science.* Newbury Park, CA: Sage.

Gudykunst, W. B. (1988). Uncertainty and anxiety. In Y. Y. Kim & W. B. Gudykunst (Eds.), *Theories in intercultural communication.* Newbury Park, CA: Sage.

Gudykunst, W. B. (1989). Culture and the development of interpersonal relationships. In J. A. Anderson (Ed.), *Communication yearbook 12.* Newbury Park, CA: Sage.

Gudykunst, W. B. (1991). *Bridging differences.* Newbury Park, CA: Sage.

Gudykunst, W. B. (Ed.) (1993a). *Communication in Japan and the United States.* Albany: State University of New York Press.

Gudykunst, W. B. (1993b). Toward a theory of effective interpersonal and intergroup communication: An anxiety/uncertainty management (AUM) perspective. In R. L. Wiseman & J. Koester (Eds.), *Intercultural communication competence.* Newbury Park, CA: Sage.

Gudykunst, W. B., Gao, G., Nishida, T., Nadamitsu, Y., & Sakai, J. (1992). Self-monitoring in Japan and the United States. In S. Iwaki, Y. Kashima, & K. Leung (Eds.), *Innovations in cross-cultural psychology.* The Hague, The Netherlands: Swets & Zeitlinger.

Gudykunst, W. B. (1994). *Bridging differences* (2nd. ed.). Thousand Oaks, CA: Sage.

Gudykunst, W. B., Gao, G., Schmidt, K., Nishida, T., Bond, M. H., Leung, K., Wang, G., & Barraclough, R. A. (1992). The influence of individualism-collectivism on communication in ingroup and outgroup relationships. *Journal of Cross-Cultural Psychology, 23,* 196-213.

Gudykunst, W. B., Gao, G., Sudweeks, S., Ting-Toomey, S., & Nishida, T. (1991). Themes in opposite sex, Japanese-North American relationships. In S. Ting-Toomey & F. Korzenny (Eds.), *Cross-cultural interpersonal communication.* Newbury Park, CA: Sage.

Gudykunst, W. B., & Kim, Y. Y. (1984). *Communicating with strangers.* Reading, MA: Addison-Wesley.

Gudykunst, W. B., & Nishida, T. (1983). Social penetration in Japanese and American close friendships. In R. Bostrom (Ed.), *Communication yearbook 7.* Beverly Hills, CA: Sage.

Gudykunst, W. B., & Nishida, T. (1984). Individual and cultural influences on uncertainty reduction. *Communication Monographs, 51,* 23-36.

Gudykunst, W. B., & Nishida, T. (1986a). Attributional confidence in low- and high-context cultures. *Human Communication Research, 12,* 525-549.

Gudykunst, W. B., & Nishida, T. (1986b). The influence of cultural variability on perceptions of communication behavior associated with relationship terms. *Human Communication Research, 13,* 147-166.

Gudykunst, W. B., & Nishida, T. (1993). Relationship closeness in Japan and the United States. *Research in Social Psychology, 8*(2), 85-97.

Gudykunst, W. B., Nishida, T., & Chua, E. (1986). Uncertainty reduction in Japanese-North American dyads. *Communication Research Reports, 3,* 39-46.

Gudykunst, W. B., Nishida, T., & Chua, E. (1987). Perceptions of social penetration in Japanese-North American dyads. *International Journal of Intercultural Relations, 11,* 171-189.

Gudykunst, W. B., Nishida, T., Chung, L., & Sudweeks, S. (1992). *The influence of strength of cultural identity and perceived typicality on individualistic and collectivistic values in Japan and the United States.* Paper presented at the Asian Regional Congress of the International Association for Cross-Cultural Psychology, Kathmandu, Nepal.

Gudykunst, W. B., Nishida, T., & Morisaki, S. (1992). *The influence of cultural and social identity on the evaluation of interpersonal and intergroup encounters in the United States.* Paper presented at the International Communication Association convention, Miami.

Gudykunst, W. B., Nishida, T., & Schmidt, K. L. (1989). Cultural, relational, and personality influences on uncertainty reduction processes. *Western Speech Communication Journal, 53,* 13-29.

Gudykunst, W. B,, & Ting-Toomey, S., with Chua, E. (1988). *Culture and interpersonal communication.* Newbury Park, CA: Sage.

Gudykunst, W. B., Yang, S. M., & Nishida, T. (1985). A cross-cultural test of uncertainty reduction theory. *Human Communication Research, 11,* 407-454.

Gudykunst, W. B., Yang, S. M., & Nishida, T. (1987). Cultural differences in self-consciousness and self-monitoring. *Communication Research, 14,* 7-36.

Gudykunst, W. B., Yoon, Y. C., & Nishida, T. (1987). The influence of individualism-collectivism on perceptions of communication in ingroup and outgroup relationships. *Communication Monographs, 54,* 295-306.

Gumperz, J. (1982). *Discourse strategies.* New York: Cambridge University Press.

Hall, E. T. (1976). *Beyond culture.* New York: Doubleday.

Hall, E. T., & Hall, M. (1987). *Hidden differences: Doing business with the Japanese.* Garden City, NY: Doubleday.

Hamaguchi, E. (1982). *Nihonteki shuhdanshugi towa nanika* [What is the Japanese groupism]. In E. Hamaguchi & S. Kumon (Ed.), *Nihonteki shudanshugi* [Japanese groupism]. Tokyo: Yuhikaku (Sensho).

Hamaguchi, E. (1983). *Kanjin-shugi no shakai Nihon* [Japan, society of contextual men]. Tokyo: Touyou Keizai.

Hamaguchi, E. (1985). A contextual model of the Japanese. *Journal of Japanese Studies, 11*(2), 289-321.

Hamilton, V., Blumenfeld, P., Akoh, H., & Miura, K. (1991). Group and gender in Japanese and American elementary classrooms. *Journal of Cross-Cultural Psychology, 22,* 317-346.

Hayashi, R. (1988). Simultaneous talk—from the perspective of floor management of English and Japanese speakers. *World Englishes, 7,* 269-288.

Hayashi, R. (1990). Rhythmicity, sequence and synchrony of English and Japanese face-to-face conversations. *Language Sciences, 12,* 155-195.

Hecht, M. (1978). The conceptualization and measurement of communication satisfaction. *Human Communication Research, 4,* 253-264.

Heider, F. (1958). *The psychology of interpersonal relations.* New York: John Wiley.

Helm, L. (1991, October 25). Japan's rising scorn for America. *Los Angeles Times,* pp. A1, A14-15.

Herman, S., & Schield, E. (1960). The stranger group in a cross-cultural situation. *Sociometry, 24,* 165-176.

Hewstone, M., & Brown, R. (1986). Contact is not enough. In M. Hewstone & R. Brown (Eds.), *Contact and conflict in intergroup encounters*. Oxford, UK: Basil Blackwell.

Hewstone, M., & Giles, H. (1986). Stereotypes and intergroup communication. In W. B. Gudykunst (Ed.), *Intergroup communication*. London: Edward Arnold.

Hewstone, M., & Jaspars, J. (1984). Social dimensions of attributions. In H. Tajfel (Ed.), *The social dimension* (Vol. 2). Cambridge, UK: Cambridge University Press.

Hildebrandt, N., & Giles, H. (1980). The English language in Japan: A social psychological perspective. *JALT Journal, 2*, 63-87.

Hillenbrand, B. (1992, February 10). America in the mind of Japan. *Time*, pp. 20-23.

Hinds, J. (1983). Contrastive rhetoric: Japanese and English. *Text, 3*, 183-195.

Hirokawa, R., & Miyahara, A. (1986). A comparison of influence strategies utilized by managers in American and Japanese organizations. *Communication Quarterly, 34*, 250-265.

Hofstede, G. (1979). Value systems in forty countries. In L. Eckensberger, W. Lonner, & Y. Poortinga (Eds.), *Cross-cultural contributions to psychology*. Lisse, The Netherlands: Swets & Zeitlinger.

Hofstede, G. (1980). *Culture's consequences*. Beverly Hills, CA: Sage.

Hofstede, G. (1991). *Cultures and organizations: Software of the mind*. New York: McGraw-Hill.

Hofstede, G., & Bond, M. H. (1984). Hofstede's culture dimensions. *Journal of Cross-Cultural Psychology, 15*, 417-433.

Honne, N. (1980). Cultural pluralism in Japan. *JALT Journal, 2*, 5-29.

Howell, W. (1982). *The empathic communicator*. Belmont, CA: Wadsworth.

Hwang, J., Chase, L., & Kelly, C. (1980). An intercultural examination of communication competence. *Communication, 9*, 70-79.

Imahori, T., & Cupach, W. (1991). *A cross-cultural comparison of the interpretation and management of face*. Paper presented at the Conference on Communication in Japan and the United States, California State University, Fullerton.

Imai, M. (1981). *16 ways to avoid saying no*. Tokyo: Nihon Keizer Shimbun.

Inkeles, A. (1974). *Becoming modern*. Cambridge: Harvard University Press.

Inoue, K. (1979). Japanese. In T. Shopen (Eds.), *Languages and their speakers*. Boston: Winthrop.

Ishii, S., Thompson, C., & Klopf, D. (1990). A comparison of the assertiveness/responsiveness construct between Japanese and Americans. *Otsuma Review, 23*, 63-71.

Ito, Y. (1989a). A non-western view of the paradigm dialogues. In B. Dervin, L. Grossberg, B. J. O'Keefe,& E. Wartella (Eds.), *Rethinking communication*. Newbury Park, CA: Sage.

Ito, Y. (1989b). Socio-cultural backgrounds of Japanese interpersonal communication style. *Civilisations, 39*, 101-137.

Ito, Y. (1992). Theories on interpersonal communication styles from a Japanese perspective: A sociological perspective. In J. Blumler, J. McCleod, & K.

Rosengren (Eds.), *Comparatively speaking: Communication and culture across space and time*. Newbury Park, CA: Sage.

Izard, C. (1968). *The emotions as a culture-common framework of motivational experiences and communication*. Technical Report No. 30, Vanderbilt University Contract No. 2149(03)-NR 171-6090, Office of Naval Research.

Izard, C. (1970). *The face of emotion*. New York: Appleton-Century-Crofts.

Jackson, J. (1964). The normative regulation of authoritative behavior. In W. Grove & J. Dyson (Eds.), *The making of decisions*. New York: Free Press.

Janis, I., & Mann, L. (1977). *Decision making*. New York: Free Press.

Johnson, C., & Johnson, F. (1975). Interaction rules and ethnicity. *Social Forces, 54*, 452-466.

Johnson, S. K. (1991). *The Japanese through American eyes*. Stanford: Stanford University Press.

Jorden, E. (1977). Linguistic fraternization. In *Proceedings of the symposium on Japanese sociolinguistics*. San Antonio: Trinity University.

Kashima, Y., & Triandis, H. C. (1986). The self-serving bias in attributions as a coping strategy. *Journal of Cross-Cultural Psychology, 17*, 83-97.

Kawashima, T. (1967). *Nipponjin no ho-ishiki* [The Japanese consciousness of law]. Tokyo: Iwanami.

Keesing, R. (1974). Theories of culture. *Annual Review of Anthropology, 3*, 73-97.

Kelley, H. (1967). Attribution theory in social psychology. *Nebraska Symposium on Motivation, 15*, 192-238.

Kennerley, H. (1990). *Managing anxiety*. New York: Oxford University Press.

Kertamus, L., Gudykunst, W. B., & Nishida, T. (1991). *Relational themes in male-male, Japanese-North American relationships*. Paper presented at the Conference on Communication in Japan and the United States, California State University, Fullerton.

Kitamura, H. (1971). *Psychological dimensions of U.S.-Japanese Relations*. Cambridge, MA: Harvard University Center for International Affairs.

Kitayama, S., & Burnstein, E. (1988). Automaticity in conversations. *Journal of Personality and Social Psychology, 54*, 219-224.

Klopf, D. W. (1984). Cross-cultural apprehension research: A summary of Pacific Basin studies. In J. A. Daly & J. C. McCroskey (Eds.), *Avoiding communication: Shyness, reticence, and communication apprehension*. Beverly Hills, CA: Sage.

Klopf, D., & Cambra, R. (1981). A comparison of communication styles of Japanese and American college students. *Current English Studies, 20*, 66-71.

Kluckhohn, F., & Strodtbeck, F. (1961). *Variations in value orientations*. New York: Row, Peterson.

Knapp, M., Ellis, D., & Williams, B. (1980). Perceptions of communication behavior associated with relationship terms. *Communication Monographs, 47*, 262-278.

Kondo, D. K. (1990). *Crafting selves: Power, gender, and discourses of identity in a Japanese workplace*. Chicago: University of Chicago Press.

Krauss, E., Rohlen, T., & Steinhoff, G. (Eds.). (1984). *Conflict in Japan.* Honolulu: University of Hawaii Press.

Kumagai, F., & Strauss, M. (1983). Conflict resolution tactics in Japan, India, and the United States. *Journal of Comparative Family Studies, 14,* 337-387.

Kumon, S. (1982). *Soshiki no Nihongata moderu to obeigata moderu* [Japanese and American models of organizations]. In E. Hamaguchi & S. Kumon (Eds.), *Nihonteki shuhdanshugi* [Japanese groupism]. Tokyo: Yuhikaku (Sensho).

Kunihiro, M. (1976, Winter). Indigenous barriers to communication. *Japan Interpreter*, pp. 96-108.

Langer, E. (1978). Rethinking the role of thought in social interaction. In J. Harvey, W. Ickes, & R. Kidd (Eds.), *New directions in attribution research* (Vol. 2). Hillsdale, NJ: Lawrence Erlbaum.

Langer, E. (1989). *Mindfulness.* Reading, MA: Addison-Wesley.

Lebra, T. S. (1974). Reciprocity and the asymmetrical principle. In T. Lebra & W. Lebra (Eds), *Japanese culture and behavior.* Honolulu: University of Hawaii Press.

Lebra, T. S. (1976). *Japanese patterns of behavior.* Honolulu: University of Hawaii Press.

Lebra, T. S. (1984). *Japanese women.* Honolulu: University of Hawaii Press.

Lebra, T. S. (1987). The cultural significance of silence in Japanese communication. *Multilingua, 6,* 343-357.

Levine, D. (1985). *The flight from ambiguity.* Chicago: University of Chicago Press.

Levine, R., & Campbell, D. (1972). *Ethnocentrism.* New York: John Wiley.

LoCastro, V. (1987). *Aizuchi:* A Japanese conversational routine. In L. Smith (Ed.), *Discourse across cultures.* Englewood Cliffs, NJ: Prentice Hall.

Loveday, L. (1982). Communicative interference. *International Review of Applied Linguistics in Language Teaching, 20,* 1-16.

Lukens, J. (1978). Ethnocentric speech. *Ethnic Groups, 2,* 35-53.

Maeda, S. (1969). *Hitomishiri* [Stranger anxiety]. *Seshin Bunseki Kenkyu* (Japanese Journal of Psychoanalysis), *15*(2), 16-19.

Markus, H., & Kitayama, S. (1991). Culture and the self: Implications for cognition, emotion, and motivation. *Psychological Review, 98,* 224-253.

Maslow, A. H. (1971). *The farther reaches of human nature.* New York: Viking.

Matsumoto, M. (1988). *The unspoken way.* Tokyo: Kodansha.

Matsumoto, D., Kudoh, T., Scherer, K., & Wallbott, H. (1988). Antecedents of and reactions to emotions in Japan and the United States. *Journal of Cross-Cultural Psychology, 19,* 267-286.

Maynard, S. (1986). On back-channel behavior in Japanese and English casual conversations. *Linguistics, 24,* 85-114.

Midooka, K. (1990). Characteristics of Japanese-style communication. *Media, Culture, and Society, 12,* 477-489.

Miller, G., & Steinberg, M. (1975). *Between people.* Chicago: Science Research Associates.

Miller, G., & Sunnafrank, M. (1982). All is for one but one is not for all: A conceptual perspective of interpersonal communication. In F. Dance (Ed.), *Human communication theory*. New York: Harper & Row.

Miller, R. (1977). *The Japanese language in contemporary Japan*. Stanford: Hoover Institute.

Minamoto, R. (1969). *Giri to ninjo* [Obligation and human feeling]. Tokyo: Chuo Koronsha.

Miyahira, K. (1991). *Need profiles of intercultural communication competence in Japanese-American student dyads*. Paper presented at the Conference on Communication in Japan and the United States, California State University, Fullerton.

Miyanaga, K. (1991). *The creative edge: Individualism in Japan*. New Brunswick, NJ: Transaction Books.

Mizutani, O. (1981). *Japanese: The spoken language in Japanese life*. Tokyo: Japan Times.

Mizutani, O, & Mizutani, N. (1987). *How to be polite in Japanese*. Tokyo: Japan Times.

Morisaki, S., & Gudykunst, W. B. (in press). Face in Japan and the United States. In S. Ting-Toomey (Ed.), *The challenge of facework*. Albany: State University of New York Press.

Morsbach, H. (1988a). Nonverbal communication and hierarchical relationships. In F. Payatos (Ed.), *Cross-cultural perspectives in nonverbal communication*. Toronto: C. J. Hogrefe.

Morsbach, H. (1988b). The importance of silence and stillness in Japanese nonverbal communication. In F. Payatos (Ed.), *Cross-cultural perspectives on nonverbal communication*. Toronto: C. J. Hogrefe.

Murase, T. (1984). *Sunao*: A central concept in Japanese psychotherapy. In A. Marsella & G. White (Eds.), *Cultural conceptions of mental health and therapy*. New York: Reidel.

Murrow, L. (1992, February 10). Japan in the mind of America. *Time*, pp. 16-20.

Mushakoji, K. (1976). The cultural premises of Japanese diplomacy. In Japan Center for Education Exchange (Ed.), *The silent power*. Tokyo: Simul Press.

Nakamura, H. (1967). Consciousness of the individual and the universal among the Japanese. In C. Moore (Ed.), *The Japanese mind*. Honolulu: East West Center Press.

Nakamura, H. (1968). Basic features of the legal, political, and economic thought of Japanese. In C. Moore (Ed.), *Philosophy and culture*. Honolulu: University of Hawii Press.

Nakamura, M. (1990). *Daigakusei no yujinkankei no hattenkatei ni kansuru kenkyu - Kankeikanyosei o yosokusuru shakai kokanmoderu no hikakukento* [A study of the developmental processes of friendship in college students: A comparative examination of social exchange models predicting relationship commitment]. *Shakaishinrigaku Kenkyu* [Research in Social Psychology], 5, 29-41.

Nakane, C. (1970). *Japanese society*. Berkeley: University of California Press.

Nakane, C. (1974). The social system reflected in interpersonal communication. In J. Condon & M. Saito (Eds.), *Intercultural encounters with Japan*. Tokyo: Simul Press.

Nakanishi, M. (1986). Perceptions of self-disclosure in initial interactions: A Japanese sample. *Human Communication Research, 13*, 167-190.

Nakanishi, M., & Johnson, K. M. (1993). Implications of self-disclosure on conversational logics, perceived communication competence, and social attraction: A comparison of Japanese and American cultures. In R. L. Wiseman & J. Koester (Eds.), *Intercultural communication competence*. Newbury Park, CA: Sage.

Naotsuka, R., & Sakamoto, N. (1981). *Mutual understanding of different cultures*. Osaka, Japan: Science Education Institute.

Neuberg, S. (1989). The goal of forming accurate impressions. *Journal of Personality and Social Psychology, 56*, 374-386.

Neulip, J., & Hazelton, V. (1985). A cross-cultural comparison of Japanese and American persuasive strategy selection. *International Journal of Intercultural Relations, 9*, 389-404.

Neustupny, J. V. (1987). *Communicating with the Japanese*. Tokyo: Japan Times.

Nishida, H. (1981). Value orientations and value changes in Japan and the U.S.A. In T. Nishida & W. B. Gudykunst (Eds.), *Readings in intercultural communication*. Tokyo: Geirinshobo.

Nishida, H., & Nishida, T. (1978). *Giri and its influence on Japanese interpersonal communication*. Paper presented at the Speech Communication Association Summer Conference on International and Intercultural Communication, Tampa, FL.

Nishida, T. (1977). An analysis of a cultural concept affecting Japanese interpersonal communication. *Communication, 6*, 69-80.

Nishida, T. (1988). *Daigakusei no komyunikeishon fuan* [Communication apprehension among Japanese college students]. *"Kokusaikankei Kenkyu" Nihon Daigaku* [Nihon University Studies on International Relations], *8* (3), 171-183.

Nishida, T. (1991). *Sequence patterns of self-disclosure among Japanese and North American students*. Paper presented at the Conference on Communication in Japan and the United States, California State University, Fullerton.

Nisugi, M. (1974). Images of spoken Japanese and spoken English. In J. Condon & M. Saito (Eds.), *Intercultural encounters with Japan*. Tokyo: Simul.

Nomura, N., & Barnlund, D. (1983). Patterns of interpersonal criticism in Japan and the United States. *International Journal of Intercultural Relations, 7*, 1-8.

Norton, R. (1978). Foundations of a communicator style construct. *Human Communication Research, 4*, 99-112.

Ohbuchi, K. I., & Kitanaga, T. (1991). Effectiveness of power strategies in interpersonal conflict among Japanese students. *Journal of Social Psychology, 131*, 791-805.

Okabe, R. (1983). Cultural assumptions of East and West: Japan and the United States. In W. B. Gudykunst (Ed.), *Intercultural communication theory: Current perspectives*. Beverly Hills, CA: Sage.

Patridge, K., & Shibano, M. (1991). *Assertiveness in Japan: Individualism in a collectivistic culture*. Paper presented at the Conference on Individualism-Collectivism, Seoul, Korea.

Peng, F. (1974). Communicative distance. *Language Sciences, 31*, 32-38.

Peterson, R., & Shimada, J. (1978). Sources of management problems in Japanese-American joint ventures. *Academy of Management Review, 3*, 796-804.

Pettigrew, T. (1979). The ultimate attribution error. *Personality and Social Psychology Bulletin, 5*, 461-476.

Pharr, S. J. (1990). *Losing face: Status politics in Japan*. Berkeley: University of California Press.

Plummer, K. (1992). *The Shogun's reluctant ambassadors: Japanese sea drifters in the North Pacific*. Portland: Oregon Historical Society.

Powers, W. G., & Lowry, D. N. (1984). Basic communication fidelity: A fundamental approach. In R. N. Bostrom (Ed.), *Competence in communication: A multidisciplinary approach*. Beverly Hills, CA: Sage.

Prather, H. (1986). *Notes on how to live in the world and still be happy*. New York: Doubleday.

Prunty, A., Klopf, D., & Ishii, S. (1990). Japanese and American tendencies to argue. *Psychological Reports, 66*, 802 (also published in *Communication Research Reports*, 1990, 7, 75-79).

Reynolds, D. (1976). *Morita psychotherapy*. Berkeley: University of California Press.

Rohlen, T. (1973). Spiritual education in a Japanese bank. *American Anthropologist, 75*, 1542-1562.

Rosenberger, N. (Ed.). (1992). *Japanese sense of self*. New York: Cambridge University Press.

Ross, L. D. (1977). The intuitive psychologist and his shortcomings. In L. Berkowitz (Ed.), *Advances in experimental psychology* (Vol. 10). New York: Academic Press.

Ruben, B. D., & Kealey, D. (1979). Behavioral assessment of communication competency and the prediction of cross-cultural adaptation. *International Journal of Intercultural Relations, 3*, 15-48.

Saint-Jacques, B. (1983). Language attitudes in contemporary Japan. *Japan Foundation Newsletter, 11*, 7-14.

San Antonio, P. (1987). Social mobility and language usage in an American company in Japan. *Journal of Language and Social Psychology, 6*, 191-200.

Sato, K., Mauro, R., & Tucker, J. (1990). *A cross-cultural examination of the cognitive dimension of human emotions*. Paper presented at the Congress of the International Association for Cross-Cultural Psychology, Nara, Japan.

Simmons, D., Vom Kolke, A., & Shimuzu, H. (1986). Attitudes toward romantic love among Americans, Germans, and Japanese. *Journal of Social Psychology, 126*, 327-336.

Smith, R. J. (1983). *Japanese society.* Cambridge, UK: Cambridge University Press.

Sorrentino, R. M., & Short, J. A. (1986). Uncertainty orientation, motivation, and cognition. In R. Sorrentino & E. Higgins (Eds.), *The handbook of motivation and cognition.* New York: Guilford.

Spitzberg, B., & Cupach, W. (1984). *Interpersonal communication competence.* Beverly Hills, CA: Sage.

Stephan, W. (1985). Intergroup relations. In G. Lindzey & E. Aronson (Eds.), *Handbook of Social Psychology* (3rd ed., Vol. 2). New York: Random House.

Stephan, W., & Rosenfield, D. (1982). Racial and ethnic stereotyping. In A. Millar (Ed.), *In the eye of the beholder.* New York: Praeger.

Stephan, W., & Stephan, C. (1985). Intergroup anxiety. *Journal of Social Issues, 41,* 157-166.

Stephan, W., & Stephan, C. (1989). Antecedants of intergroup anxiety in Asian-Americans and Hispanic-Americans. *International Journal of Intercultural Relations, 13,* 203-219.

Sudweeks, S., Gudykunst, W. B., Ting-Toomey, S., & Nishida, T. (1990). Developmental themes in Japanese-North American interpersonal relationships. *International Journal of Intercultural Relations, 14,* 207-233.

Sueda, K., & Wiseman, R. (1992). A cross-cultural study of embarrassment: The United States and Japanese cultures. *International Journal of Intercultural Relations, 16,* 159-174.

Sumner, W. G. (1940). *Folkways.* Boston: Ginn.

Sussman, N., & Rosenfeld, H. (1982). Influence of culture, language, and sex on conversational distance. *Journal of Personality and Social Psychology, 42,* 66-74.

Suzuki, T. (1978). *Words in context.* Tokyo: Kodansha.

Tada, M. (1958). *Haji to taimen* [Shame and face]. In *Gendai rinri* [Contemporary ethics] (Vol. 6). Tokyo: Chikuna Shoboo.

Tajfel, H. (1978). Social categorization, social identity, and social comparisons. In H. Tajfel (Ed.), *Differentiation between social groups.* London: Academic Press.

Takabayashi, S. (1986). Japanese philosophy and general semantics. *Et cetera, 43,* 181-190.

Takahara, N. (1974). Semantic concepts of marriage, work, friendship, and foreigner in three cultures. In J. Condon & M. Saito (Eds.), *Intercultural encounters with Japan.* Tokyo: Simul Press.

Tannen, D. (1979). Ethnicity and conversational style. In *Working papers on sociolinguistics* (Number 55). Austin, TX: Southwest Educational Development Laboratory.

Tezuka, C. (1992). *Awase* and *sunao* and their implications for Japanese and American cross-cultural communication. *Keio Communication Review, 14,* 37-50.

Thakerar, J., & Iwawaki, S. (1979). Cross-cultural comparisons in interpersonal attraction of females toward males. *Journal of Social Psychology, 108,* 121-122.

Ting-Toomey, S. (1985). Toward a theory of conflict and culture. In W. B.
    Gudykunst, L. P. Stewart, & S. Ting-Toomey (Eds.), *Communication,
    culture, and organizational processes*. Beverly Hills, CA: Sage.
Ting-Toomey, S. (1986). Japanese communication patterns: Insider versus the
    outsider. *World Communication, 15*, 113-126.
Ting-Toomey, S. (1988a). Intercultural conflict styles: A face-negotiation the-
    ory. In Y. Y. Kim & W. B. Gudykunst (Eds.), *Theories in intercultural
    communication*. Newbury Park, CA: Sage.
Ting-Toomey, S. (1988b). Rhetorical sensitivity style in three cultures: France,
    Japan, and the United States. *Central States Speech Journal, 39*, 28-36.
Ting-Toomey, S. (1991). Intimacy expressions in three cultures: France, Japan,
    and the United States. *International Journal of Intercultural Relations,
    15*, 29-46.
Ting-Toomey, S. (1994). Managing intercultural conflicts effectively. In L.
    Samovar & R. Porter (Eds.), *Intercultural communication: A reader* (7th
    ed.). Belmont, CA: Wadsworth.
Ting-Toomey, S., & Gao, G. (1988). Intercultural adaptation process in Japan:
    Perceived similarity, self-consciousness, and language competence. *World
    Communication, 17*, 193-206.
Ting-Toomey, S., Trubisky, P., & Nishida, T. (1989). *Conflict resolution styles
    in Japan and the United States*. Paper presented at the Speech Commu-
    nication Association Convention, San Francisco.
Triandis, H. C. (1977). *Interpersonal behavior*. Monterey, CA: Brooks/Cole.
Triandis, H. C. (1988). Collectivism vs. individualism: A reconceptualization of
    a basic concept in cross-cultural psychology. In G. Verma & C. Bagley
    (Eds.), *Cross-cultural studies of personality, attitudes and cognition*.
    London: Macmillan.
Triandis, H. C., Bontempo, R., Villareal, M., Asai, M., & Lucca, N. (1988).
    Individualism-collectivism: Cross-cultural perspectives on self-ingroup re-
    lationships. *Journal of Personality and Social Psychology, 54*, 323-338.
Triandis, H. C., Brislin, R. W., & Hui, C. H. (1988). Cross-cultural training across
    the individualism-collectivism divide. *International Journal of Intercul-
    tural Relations, 12*, 269-289.
Tsuda, Y. (1986). *Language inequality and distortion*. Amsterdam: John
    Benjamins.
Tsujimura, A. (1987). Some characteristics of the Japanese way of communica-
    tion. In D. L. Kincaid (Ed.), *Communication theory from eastern and
    western perspectives*. New York: Academic Press.
Turner, J. H. (1988). *A theory of social interaction*. Stanford, CA: Stanford
    University Press.
Ueda, K. (1974). Sixteen ways to avoid saying "no" in Japan. In J. Condon & M.
    Saito (Eds.), *Intercultural encounters with Japan*. Tokyo: Simul.
United States-Japan Advisory Commission (1984). *Challenges and opportuni-
    ties in United States-Japan relations*. A report submitted to the Presi-
    dent of the United States and the Prime Minister of Japan.
van Dijk, T. (1984). *Prejudice in discourse*. Amsterdam: Benjamins.
Vogel, E. (1963). *Japan's new middle class*. Berkeley: University of California
    Press.

Wallace, A. (1952). Individual differences and cultural uniformities. *American Sociological Review, 17*, 747-750.

Waterman, A. (1984). *The psychology of individualism*. New York: Praeger.

Watson, D., Clark, L., & Tellegen, A. (1984). Cross-cultural convergence in the structure of mood: A Japanese replication and a comparison with U.S. findings. *Journal of Personality and Cross-Cultural Psychology, 47*, 127-144.

Watzlawick, P., Beavin, J., & Jackson, D. (1967). *The pragmatics of human communication*. New York: Norton.

Wetzel, P. (1985). In-group/out-group deixis: Situation variation in the verbs of giving and receiving. In J. Forgas (Ed.), *Language and social situations*. New York: Springer Verlag.

White, M. (1993). *The material child: Coming of age in Japan and the United States*. New York: Basic Books.

White, S. (1989). Back channels across cultures: A study of Americans and Japanese. *Language in Society, 18*, 59-76.

Whorf, B. L. (1956). *Language, thought, and reality*. New York: John Wiley.

Wiemann, J., Chen, V., & Giles, H. (1986). *Beliefs about talk and silence in cultural context*. Paper presented at the Speech Communication Association Convention, Chicago.

Wiemann, J., & Kelly, C. (1981). Pragmatics of interpersonal competence. In C. Wilder-Mott & J. Weaklund (Eds.), *Rigor and imagination*. New York: Praeger.

Wierzbica, A. (1991). Japanese key words and cultural values. *Language in Society, 20*, 333-385.

Wilder, D. A., & Shapiro, P. (1989). Effects of anxiety on impression formation in a group context. *Journal of Experimental Social Psychology, 25*, 481-499.

Williams, T., & Sogon, S. (1984). *Nihonjin daigakusei niokeru shudankeisei to tekio kodo* [Group composition and conforming behavior in Japanese students]. *Nihon Shinrigaku Kenkyu* [Japanese Psychological Research], *126*, 231-234.

Wiseman, S. R. (1991, December 8). Japanese think they owe apology and are owed one on war, poll shows. *New York Times*, p. Y16.

Wuthnow, R. (1991). *Acts of compassion: Caring for others and helping ourselves*. Princeton: Princeton University Press.

Yamada, H. (1990). Topic management and turn distributions in business meetings: American versus Japanese strategies. *Text, 10*, 271-295.

Yamada, H. (in press). *Topic management strategies in American and Japanese business meetings*. Norwood, NJ: Ablex.

Yamaguchi, S. (1990). *Empirical evidence on collectivism among the Japanese*. Paper presented at the Conference on Individualism-Collectivism, Seoul, Korea.

Yamaguchi, S. (1991). *"Jiko" no shitenkara no shudan oyobi bunkasa eno apurochi* [An approach to group processes and cultural differences from the perspective of the self]. *Shakaishinrigaku Kenkyu* [Research in Social Psychology], *6*, 138-147.

Yamazaki, M. (1985). *Yawarakai kojinshugi no tanjo* [The birth of modern individualism]. Tokyo: Chukoronsha.

Yamazaki, M. (1990). *Nihonbunnka to kojinshugi* [Japanese culture and individualism]. Tokyo: Chukoronsha.

Yoneyama, T. (1973). Basic notions in Japanese social relations. In J. Bailey (Ed.), *Listening to Japan*. New York: Praeger.

Yoshikawa, M. (1978). Some Japanese and American cultural characteristics. In M. Prosser, *The cultural dialogue*. Boston: Houghton Mifflin.

Yoshima, T., & Sasatami, T. (1980). The teaching of English in upper secondary schools in Miyazaki prefecture. *Memoirs of the Faculty of Education* (Vol. 47), Miyazaki University.

Yoshino, K. (1992). *Cultural nationalism in Japan*. New York: Routledge.

Yum, J. O. (1988). The impact of Confucianism in interpersonal relationships and conmmunication in East Asia. *Communication Monographs, 55*, 374-388.

Zander, A. (1983). The value of belonging to a group in Japan. *Small Group Behavior, 14*, 3-14.

Author Index

Subject Index

About the Authors

William B. Gudykunst is Professor of Speech Communication at California State University, Fullerton. He became interested in Japanese/North American communication when he was an Intercultural Relations Specialist with the U.S. Navy in Yokosuka, Japan. The focus of his work is on developing a theory to explain effective interpersonal and intergroup communication, with a special emphasis on communication between people from Japan and the United States. He has written several books on the topic, including *Bridging Differences* (translated into Japanese), *Communicating With Strangers* (with Young Yun Kim), and *Culture and Interpersonal Communication* (with Stella Ting-Toomey). He also has edited several books, including *Communication in Japan and the United States*, *Intergroup Communication*, and *Handbook of International and Intercultural Communication* (with Molefi K. Asante).

Tsukasa Nishida is Professor of Intercultural Relations at Nihon University in Mishima, Japan. He became interested in Japanese/North American communication when he started graduate work in speech communication in the United States. The focus of his work is on human relations in Japan and the United States. He has written several books in Japanese on intercultural communication, including *Human Relation Rules in the U.S.A.*, *A Study of Intercultural Behavior*, and *American Communication Patterns* (with Hiroko Nishida). He has edited

Culture Shock: Surprise! This Is Japan, *A Study of Internation-
Human Relations*, and *Readings in Intercultural Communic-
tion* (with William B. Gudykunst). He has translated sever
books into Japanese, including *Bridging Differences*, *Unde-
standing Intercultural Communication*, and *Silent Message*